The Root of the Righteous

by A. W. Tozer

§

CHRISTIAN PUBLICATIONS, INC.

HARRISBURG, PA.

Contents

Preface 5

The Root of the Righteous 7

We Must Give Time to God 10

God Is Easy to Live With 13

Listen to the Man Who Listens to God 17

We Must Hear Worthily 19

That Utilitarian Christ 23

On Receiving Admonition 27

The Great God Entertainment 30

Bible Taught or Spirit Taught? 34

The Terror of the Lord 38

No Regeneration Without Reformation 42

Faith Is a Perturbing Thing 45

True Faith Brings Committal 49

The Great Disparity 51

Our Enemy Contentment 54

Christ Is the Pattern 57

The Cross Is a Radical Thing 61

We Must Die If We Would Live 64

Christ Died for Our Hearts 67

We Stand in Christ's Triumph 70

To Be or To Do 73

Make Room for Mystery 77

The Whole Life Must Pray 81

No Saviourhood Without Lordship 83

"A Sweet Lute, Sweetly Played" 87

The All-importance of Motive 89

The Presence More Important Than the Program .. 92

The World's Most Tragic Waste 96

The Hunger of the Wilderness 100

Our Fruit Will Be What We Are 103

Needed: A Baptism of Clear Seeing 107

Narrow Mansions 111

The Sanctification of Our Desires 115

In Praise of Disbelief 119

Thankfulness As a Moral Therapeutic 122

Understanding Those Dry Spells 126

About Hindrances 128

The Uses of Suffering 131

Praise God for the Furnace 134

Victory in the Guise of Defeat 138

Love of the Unseen Is Possible 141

Something Beyond Song 144

Three Degrees of Love 147

We Need Cool Heads 150

We Can Afford to Wait 154

God, the First and the Last 158

Preface

These chapters came into being over a period of about five years and were written in many places and under a variety of interesting circumstances. They are in no sense quiet religious essays, but were born in the midst of life; and while they have, as I hope, heaven in full view, they are never too far removed from the rough world where the children of God struggle and work and pray.

The favorable reception given these chapters when they first appeared as editorials in *The Alliance Weekly* led to their publication in this more permanent form.

A. W. T.

The Root of the Righteous

One marked difference between the faith of our
fathers as conceived by the fathers and the same faith
as understood and lived by their children is that the
fathers were concerned with the root of the matter,
while their present-day descendants seem concerned
only with the fruit.

This appears in our attitude toward certain great
Christian souls whose names are honored among the
churches, as, for instance, Augustine and Bernard in
earlier times, or Luther and Wesley in times more
recent. Today we write the biographies of such as
these and celebrate their fruit, but the tendency is to
ignore the root out of which the fruit sprang. "The
root of the righteous yieldeth fruit," said the wise man
in the Proverbs. Our fathers looked well to the root
of the tree and were willing to wait with patience for
the fruit to appear. We demand the fruit immediately
even though the root may be weak and knobby or
missing altogether. Impatient Christians today explain
away the simple beliefs of the saints of other days

and smile off their serious-minded approach to God and sacred things. They were victims of their own limited religious outlook, but great and sturdy souls withal who managed to achieve a satisfying spiritual experience and do a lot of good in the world in spite of their handicaps. So we'll imitate their fruit without accepting their theology or inconveniencing ourselves too greatly by adopting their all-or-nothing attitude toward religion.

So we say (or more likely think without saying), and every voice of wisdom, every datum of religious experience, every law of nature tells us how wrong we are. The bough that breaks off from the tree in a storm may bloom briefly and give to the unthinking passer-by the impression that it is a healthy and fruitful branch, but its tender blossoms will soon perish and the bough itself wither and die. There is no lasting life apart from the root.

Much that passes for Christianity today is the brief bright effort of the severed branch to bring forth its fruit in its season. But the deep laws of life are against it. Preoccupation with appearances and a corresponding neglect of the out-of-sight root of the true spiritual life are prophetic signs which go unheeded. Immediate "results" are all that matter, quick proofs of present success without a thought of next week or next year. Religious pragmatism is running wild among the orthodox. Truth is whatever works.

If it gets results it is good. There is but one test for the religious leader: success. Everything is forgiven him except failure.

A tree can weather almost any storm if its root is sound, but when the fig tree which our Lord cursed "dried up from the roots" it immediately "withered away." A church that is soundly rooted cannot be destroyed, but nothing can save a church whose root is dried up. No stimulation, no advertising campaigns, no gifts of money and no beautiful edifice can bring back life to the rootless tree.

With a happy disregard for consistency of metaphor the Apostle Paul exhorts us to look to our sources. "Rooted and grounded in love," he says in what is obviously a confusion of figure; and again he urges his readers to be "rooted and built up in him," which envisages the Christian both as a tree to be well rooted and as a temple to rise on a solid foundation.

The whole Bible and all the great saints of the past join to tell us the same thing. "Take nothing for granted," they say to us. "Go back to the grass roots. Open your hearts and search the Scriptures. Bear your cross, follow your Lord and pay no heed to the passing religious vogue. The masses are always wrong. In every generation the number of the righteous is small. Be sure you are among them."

"A man shall not be established by wickedness: but the root of the righteous shall not be moved."

We Must Give Time to God

Probably the most widespread and persistent problem to be found among Christians is the problem of retarded spiritual progress. Why, after years of Christian profession, do so many persons find themselves no farther along than when they first believed?

Some would try to resolve the difficulty by asserting flatly that such persons were never saved, that they had never been truly regenerated. They are simply deceived professors who have stopped short of true conversion.

With a few this may be the answer, and we would accept this explanation as final did we not know that it is never the deceived professor who laments his lack of spiritual growth, but the true Christian who has had a real experience of conversion and who is sure that he is this very moment trusting in Christ for salvation. Uncounted numbers of such believers are among the disappointed ones who deplore their failure to make progress in the spiritual life.

The causes of retarded growth are many. It would not be accurate to ascribe the trouble to one single fault. One there is, however, which is so universal that it may easily be the main cause: *failure to give time to the cultivation of the knowledge of God.*

The temptation to make our relation to God judicial instead of personal is very strong. Believing for salvation has these days been reduced to a once-done act that requires no further attention. The young believer becomes aware of an act performed rather than of a living Saviour to be followed and adored.

The Christian is strong or weak depending upon how closely he has cultivated the knowledge of God. Paul was anything but an advocate of the once-done, automatic school of Christianity. He devoted his whole life to the art of knowing Christ. "Yea doubtless, and I count all things but loss for the excellency of the knowledge of Christ Jesus my Lord: for whom I have suffered the loss of all things, and do count them but dung, that I may win Christ. . . . That I may know him, and the power of his resurrection, and the fellowship of his sufferings, being made conformable unto his death . . . I press toward the mark for the prize of the high calling of God in Christ Jesus" (Phil. 3:8, 10, 14).

Progress in the Christian life is exactly equal to the growing knowledge we gain of the Triune God in personal experience. And such experience requires a whole life devoted to it and plenty of time spent

11

at the holy task of cultivating God. God can be known satisfactorily only as we devote time to Him. Without meaning to do it we have written our serious fault into our book titles and gospel songs. "A little talk with Jesus," we sing, and we call our books "God's Minute," or something else as revealing. The Christian who is satisfied to give God His "minute" and to have "a little talk with Jesus" is the same one who shows up at the evangelistic service weeping over his retarded spiritual growth and begging the evangelist to show him the way out of his difficulty.

We may as well accept it: there is no short cut to sanctity. Even the crises that come in the spiritual life are usually the result of long periods of thought and prayerful meditation. As the wonder grows more and more dazzling there is likely to occur a crisis of revolutionizing proportions. But that crisis is related to what has gone before. It is a sudden sweet explosion, an uprushing of the water that has been increasing its pressure within until we can no longer contain it. Back of it all is the slow buildup and preparation that comes from waiting upon God.

A thousand distractions would woo us away from thoughts of God, but if we are wise we will sternly put them from us and make room for the King and take time to entertain Him. Some things may be neglected with but little loss to the spiritual life, but to neglect communion with God is to hurt ourselves where we cannot afford it. God will respond to our efforts to know Him. The Bible tells us how; it is altogether a matter of how much determination we bring to the holy task.

God Is Easy to Live With

Satan's first attack upon the human race was his sly effort to destroy Eve's confidence in the kindness of God. Unfortunately for her and for us he succeeded too well. From that day, men have had a false conception of God, and it is exactly this that has cut out from under them the ground of righteousness and driven them to reckless and destructive living.

Nothing twists and deforms the soul more than a low or unworthy conception of God. Certain sects, such as the Pharisees, while they held that God was stern and austere, yet managed to maintain a fairly high level of external morality; but their righteousness was only outward. Inwardly they were "whited sepulchres," as our Lord Himself told them. Their wrong conception of God resulted in a wrong idea of worship. To a Pharisee, the service of God was a bondage which he did not love but from which he could not escape without a loss too great to bear. The God of the Pharisee was not a God easy to live with, so his religion became grim and hard and loveless. It had to be so, for our notion of God must always determine the quality of our religion.

Much Christianity since the days of Christ's flesh has also been grim and severe. And the cause has been the same—an unworthy or an inadequate view of God. Instinctively we try to be like our God, and if He is conceived to be stern and exacting, so will we ourselves be.

From a failure properly to understand God comes a world of unhappiness among good Christians even today. The Christian life is thought to be a glum, unrelieved cross-carrying under the eye of a stern Father who expects much and excuses nothing. He is austere, peevish, highly temperamental and extremely hard to please. The kind of life which springs out of such libelous notions must of necessity be but a parody on the true life in Christ.

It is most important to our spiritual welfare that we hold in our minds always a right conception of God. If we think of Him as cold and exacting we shall find it impossible to love Him, and our lives will be ridden with servile fear. If, again, we hold Him to be kind and understanding our whole inner life will mirror that idea.

The truth is that God is the most winsome of all beings and His service one of unspeakable pleasure. He is all love, and those who trust Him need never know anything but that love. He is just, indeed, and He will not condone sin; but through the blood of the everlasting covenant He is able to act toward us exactly as if we had never sinned. Toward the trusting sons of men His mercy will always triumph over justice.

The fellowship of God is delightful beyond all telling. He communes with His redeemed ones in an easy, uninhibited fellowship that is restful and healing to the soul. He is not sensitive nor selfish nor temperamental. What He is today we shall find Him tomorrow and the next day and the next year. He is not hard to please, though He may be hard to satisfy. He expects of us only what He has Himself first supplied. He is quick to mark every simple effort to please Him, and just as quick to overlook imperfections when He knows we meant to do His will. He loves us for ourselves and values our love more than galaxies of new created worlds.

Unfortunately, many Christians cannot get free from their perverted notions of God, and these notions poison their hearts and destroy their inward freedom. These friends serve God grimly, as the elder brother did, doing what is right without enthusiasm and without joy, and seem altogether unable to understand the buoyant, spirited celebration when the prodigal comes home. Their idea of God rules out the possibility of His being happy in His people, and they attribute the singing and shouting to sheer fanaticism. Unhappy souls, these, doomed to go heavily on their melancholy way, grimly determined to do right if the heavens fall and to be on the winning side in the day of judgment.

How good it would be if we could learn that God is easy to live with. He remembers our frame and knows that we are dust. He may sometimes chasten us, it is true, but even this He does with a smile, the proud, tender smile of a Father who is bursting with pleasure over an imperfect but promising son who is coming every day to look more and more like the One whose child he is.

Some of us are religiously jumpy and self-conscious because we know that God sees our every thought and is acquainted with all our ways. We need not be. God is the sum of all patience and the essence of kindly good will. We please Him most, not by frantically trying to make ourselves good, but by throwing ourselves into His arms with all our imperfections, and believing that He understands everything and loves us still.

Listen to the Man Who Listens to God

If while hearing a sermon we can fix on but one real jewel of truth we may consider ourselves well rewarded for the time we have spent.

One such gem was uncovered during a sermon which I heard some time ago. From the sermon I got one worthy sentence and no more, but it was so good that I regret that I cannot remember who the preacher was, that I might give him credit. Here is what he said, "Listen to no man who fails to listen to God."

In any group of ten persons at least nine are sure to believe that they are qualified to offer advice to others. And in no other field of human interest are people as ready to offer advice as in the field of religion and morals. Yet it is precisely in this field that the average person is least qualified to speak wisely and is capable of the most harm when he does speak. For this reason we should select our counselors carefully. And selection inevitably carries with it the idea of rejection.

David warns against the counsel of the ungodly,

and Bible history gives examples of men who made a failure of their lives because they took wrong advice. Rehoboam, for instance, listened to men who had not listened to God and the whole future of Israel was affected adversely as a consequence. The counsel of Ahithophel was an evil thing that added greatly to the iniquities of Absalom.

No man has any right to offer advice who has not first heard God speak. No man has any right to counsel others who is not ready to hear and follow the counsel of the Lord. True moral wisdom must always be an echo of God's voice. The only safe light for our path is the light which is reflected from Christ, the Light of the World.

It is especially important that young people learn whose counsel to trust. Having been in the world for such a short time they have not had much experience and must look to others for advice. And whether they know it or not, they do every day accept the opinions of others and adopt them as their own. Those who boast the loudest of their independence have picked up from someone the idea that independence is a virtue, and their very eagerness to be individualistic is the result of the influence of others. They are what they are because of the counsel they have followed.

This rule of listening only to those who have first listened to God will save us from many a snare. All

18

religious projects should be tested by it. In this period of unusual religious activity we must keep calm and well poised. Before we follow any man we should look for the oil on his forehead. We are under no spiritual obligation to aid any man in any activity that has not upon it the marks of the cross. No appeal to our sympathies, no sad stories, no shocking pictures should move us to put our money and our time into schemes promoted by persons who are too busy to listen to God.

God has His chosen men still, and they are without exception good listeners. They can hear when the Lord speaks. We may safely listen to such men. But to no others.

We Must Hear Worthily

It is carelessly assumed by most persons that when a preacher pronounces a message of truth and his words fall upon the ears of his listeners there has been a bona fide act of hearing on their part. They are assumed to have been instructed because they have listened to the Word of God. But it does not follow.

If we would be truly instructed we must be worthy to hear; or more accurately, we must hear in a worthy manner. In listening to a sermon, reading a good book or even reading the Bible itself, much may be lost to us because we are not worthy to hear the truth. That is, we have not met the moral terms required to hear the truth rightly.

The text, "So shall my word be that goeth forth out of my mouth: it shall not return unto me void" (Isa. 55:11), does not give support to the notion that God's truth is effective wherever and whenever it is preached. The lament of the Old Testament prophets was that they cried aloud unto Israel and their words were not regarded. "Because I have called, and ye refused; I have stretched out my hand, and no man regarded; but ye have set at nought all my counsel, and would none of my reproof" (Prov. 1:24, 25). Our Lord's parable of the sower and the seed is another proof that it is possible to hear truth without profit. Paul turned from the Jews with the quotation, "Hearing ye shall hear, and shall not understand" (Acts 28:26), and began his ministry to the Gentiles.

Before there can be true inward understanding of divine truth there must be a moral preparation. Our Lord made this plain in several passages in the Gospels. "At that time Jesus answered and said, I thank thee, O Father, Lord of heaven and earth, because thou hast hid these things from the wise and prudent, and hast revealed them unto babes. Even so, Father: for so it seemed good in thy sight" (Mat. 11:25, 26). The Gospel according to John is filled with the teaching that there must be a spiritual readying within the soul before there can be a real understanding of God's truth. This is summed up in John 7:17, "If any man will do his will, he shall know of the doctrine." And Paul said plainly, "But the natural man receiveth not the things of the Spirit of God: for they are foolishness unto him: neither can he know them, because they are spiritually discerned" (1 Cor. 2:14).

When considering a pastor the average church asks in effect, "Is this man worthy to speak to us?" I suppose such a question is valid, but there is another one more in keeping with the circumstances; it is, "Are we worthy to hear this man?" An attitude of humility on the part of the hearers would secure for them a great deal more light from whatever sized candle the Lord might be pleased to send them.

When a man or woman becomes worthy to hear, God sometimes talks to them through very unworthy media. Peter, as an example, was brought to repentance by the crowing of a rooster. Of course the rooster was innocent of the part he was playing, but Peter's Lord had set things up for him so that the rooster's crow could break the heart of His backslidden apostle and send him out in a flood of penitential tears. Augustine was brought to repentance by seeing a friend killed by lightning. Nicholas Hermann was converted through seeing a tree stripped of its leaves in winter. Spurgeon became a Christian after hearing a humble Methodist class leader exhort a congregation. Moody was led into a clear anointing of the Spirit through the testimony of a simple-hearted elderly lady of his acquaintance.

All these examples teach the same thing. God will speak to the hearts of those who prepare themselves to hear; and conversely, those who do not so prepare themselves will hear nothing even though the Word of God is falling upon their outer ears every Sunday.

Good hearers are as important as good preachers. We need more of both.

That Utilitarian Christ

Our Lord forewarned us that false Christs should come. Mostly we think of these as coming from the outside, but we should remember that they may also arise within the sanctuary itself.

We must be extremely careful that the Christ we profess to follow is indeed the very Christ of God. There is always danger that we may be following a Christ who is not the true Christ but one conjured up by our imagination and made in our own image.

I confess to a feeling of uneasiness about this when I observe the questionable things Christ is said to do for people these days. He is often recommended as a wonderfully obliging but not too discriminating Big Brother who delights to help us to accomplish our ends, and who further favors us by forbearing to ask any embarrassing questions about the moral and spiritual qualities of those ends.

In our eagerness to lead men to "accept Christ" we are often tempted to present for acceptance a Christ who is little more than a caricature of "that holy thing" which was conceived by the Holy Ghost, born of the Virgin Mary, to be crucified and rise the third day to take His place on the right hand of the Majesty in the heavens.

Within the past few years, for instance, Christ has been popularized by some so-called evangelicals as one who, if a proper amount of prayer were made, would help the pious prize fighter to knock another fighter unconscious in the ring. Christ is also said to help the big league pitcher to get the proper hook on his curve. In another instance He assists an athletically-minded parson to win the high jump, and still another not only to come in first in a track meet but to set a new record in the bargain. He is said also to have helped a praying businessman to beat out a competitor in a deal, to underbid a rival and to secure a coveted contract to the discomfiture of someone else who was trying to get it. He is even thought to lend succor to a praying movie actress while she plays a role so lewd as to bring the blood to the face of a professional prostitute.

Thus our Lord becomes the Christ of utility, a kind of Aladdin's lamp to do minor miracles in behalf of anyone who summons Him to do his bidding.

Apparently no one stops to consider that if Christ were to step into a prize ring and use His divine power to help one prize fighter to paralyze another He would be putting one fighter at a cruel disadvantage and violating every common instinct of fair play.

If He were to aid one businessman to the detriment of another He would be practicing favoritism and revealing a character wholly unlike the Bible picture of the real Christ. Furthermore, we would have the grotesque situation of the Lord of glory coming to the aid of an unreconstructed Adam—on Adam's terms.

All this is too horrible to contemplate, and I hope that the proponents of this modern accommodating Christ do not see the implications that lie in their shoddy doctrine. But perhaps they do see, and are willing nevertheless to offer this utilitarian Christ as the Saviour of mankind. If so, then they no longer believe in the deity nor the lordship of Christ in any proper definition of those words. Theirs is a Christ of carnal convenience, not too far removed from the gods of paganism.

The whole purpose of God in redemption is to make us holy and to restore us to the image of God. To accomplish this He disengages us from earthly ambitions and draws us away from the cheap and unworthy prizes that worldly men set their hearts upon. A holy man would not dream of asking God to help him beat an opponent or win over a competitor. He would not wish to succeed if to do so another man must fail. No man in whom the Spirit dwells could bring himself to ask the Lord to help him knock another man unconscious for filthy lucre or the plaudits of the vulgar spectators.

A Joshua fighting the battles of the Lord, a David rescuing God's Israel from the Philistines, a Washington seeking God's help against the enemy that would enslave the young America—this is up on a high level of moral and spiritual principle and in line with the purpose of God in human history. But to teach that Christ will use His sacred power to further our worldly interests is to wrong our Lord and injure our own souls.

We modern evangelicals need to learn the truths of the sovereignty of God and the lordship of Christ. God will not play along with Adam; Christ will not be used by any of Adam's selfish brood. We had better learn these things fast if this generation of young Christians is to be spared the supreme tragedy of following a Christ who is merely a Christ of convenience and not the true Lord of glory after all.

On Receiving Admonition

An odd little passage in the Book of Ecclesiastes speaks of "an old and foolish king, who will no more be admonished."

It is not hard to understand why an old king, especially if he were a foolish one, would feel that he was beyond admonition. After he had for years given orders he might easily build a self-confident psychology that simply could not entertain the notion that he should take advice from others. His word had long been law, and to him *right* had become synonymous with his will and *wrong* had come to mean anything that ran contrary to his wishes. Soon the idea that there was anyone wise enough or good enough to reprove him would not so much as enter his mind. He had to be a foolish king to let himself get caught in that kind of web, and an old king to give the web time to get so strong that he could not break it and to give him time to get used to it so that he was no longer aware of its existence.

Regardless of the moral process by which he arrived at his hardened state, the bell had already tolled for him. In every particular he was a lost man. His wizened old body still held together to provide a kind of movable tomb to house a soul already dead. Hope had long ago departed. God had left him to his fatal conceit. And soon he would die physically too, and he would die as a fool dieth.

A state of heart that rejected admonition was characteristic of Israel at various periods in her history, and these periods were invariably followed by judgment. When Christ came to the Jews He found them chuck full of that arrogant self-confidence that would not accept reproof. "We be Abraham's seed," they said coldly when He talked to them about their sins and their need of salvation. The common people heard Him and repented, but the Jewish priests had ruled the roost too long to be willing to surrender their privileged position. Like the old king, they had gotten accustomed to being right all the time. To reprove them was to insult them. They were beyond reproof.

Churches and Christian organizations have shown a tendency to fall into the same error that destroyed Israel: inability to receive admonition. After a time of growth and successful labor comes the deadly psychology of self-congratulation. Success itself becomes the cause of later failure. The leaders come to accept themselves as the very chosen of God. They are special objects of the divine favor; their success is proof enough that this is so. They must therefore be right, and anyone who tries to call them to account is instantly written off as an unauthorized meddler who should be ashamed to dare to reprove his betters.

If anyone imagines that we are merely playing with words let him approach at random any religious leader and call attention to the weaknesses and sins in his organization. Such a one will be sure to get the quick brush off, and if he dares to persist he will be confronted with reports and statistics to prove that he is dead wrong and completely out of order. "We be the seed of Abraham" will be the burden of the defense. And who would dare find fault with Abraham's seed?

Those who have already entered the state where they can no longer receive admonition are not likely to profit by this warning. After a man has gone over the precipice there is not much you can do for him; but we can place markers along the way to prevent the next traveler from going over. Here are a few:

1. Don't defend your church or your organization against criticism. If the criticism is false it can do no harm. If it is true you need to hear it and do something about it.

2. Be concerned not with what you have accomplished but over what you might have accomplished

if you had followed the Lord completely. It is better to say (and feel), "We are unprofitable servants: we have done that which was our duty to do."

3. When reproved, pay no attention to the source. Do not ask whether it is a friend or an enemy that reproves you. An enemy is often of greater value to you than a friend because he is not influenced by sympathy.

4. Keep your heart open to the correction of the Lord and be ready to receive His chastisement regardless of who holds the whip. The great saints all learned to take a licking gracefully—and that may be one reason why they were great saints.

The Great God Entertainment

A German philosopher many years ago said something to the effect that the more a man has in his own heart the less he will require from the outside; excessive need for support from without is proof of the bankruptcy of the inner man.

If this is true (and I believe it is) then the

present inordinate attachment to every form of entertainment is evidence that the inner life of modern man is in serious decline. The average man has no central core of moral assurance, no spring within his own breast, no inner strength to place him above the need for repeated psychological shots to give him the courage to go on living. He has become a parasite on the world, drawing his life from his environment, unable to live a day apart from the stimulation which society affords him.

Schleiermacher held that the feeling of dependence lies at the root of all religious worship, and that however high the spiritual life might rise it must always begin with a deep sense of a great need which only God could satisfy. If this sense of need and a feeling of dependence are at the root of natural religion it is not hard to see why the great god Entertainment is so ardently worshiped by so many. For there are millions who cannot live without amusement; life without some form of entertainment for them is simply intolerable; they look forward to the blessed relief afforded by professional entertainers and other forms of psychological narcotics as a dope addict looks to his daily shot of heroin. Without them they could not summon courage to face existence.

No one with common human feeling will object to the simple pleasures of life, nor to such harmless forms of entertainment as may help to relax the nerves and refresh the mind exhausted by toil. Such things if used with discretion may be a blessing along the way. That is one thing. The all-out devotion to entertainment as a major activity for which and by which men live is definitely something else again.

The abuse of a harmless thing is the essence of sin. The growth of the amusement phase of human life to such fantastic proportions is a portent, a threat to the souls of modern men. It has been built into a multimillion dollar racket with greater power over human minds and human character than any other educational influence on earth. And the ominous thing is that its power is almost exclusively evil, rotting the inner life, crowding out the long eternal thoughts which would fill the souls of men if they were but worthy to entertain them. And the whole thing has grown into a veritable religion which holds its devotees with a strange fascination, and a religion, incidentally, against which it is now dangerous to speak.

For centuries the Church stood solidly against every form of worldly entertainment, recognizing it for what it was—a device for wasting time, a refuge from the disturbing voice of conscience, a scheme to divert attention from moral accountability. For this she got herself abused roundly by the sons of this world. But of late she has become tired of the abuse and has given over the struggle. She appears to have decided that if she cannot conquer the great god Entertainment she may as well join forces with him and make what use she can of his powers. So today we have the astonishing spectacle of millions of dollars being poured into the unholy job of providing earthly entertainment for the so-called sons of heaven. Religious entertainment is in many places rapidly crowding out the serious things of God. Many churches these days have become little more than poor theatres where fifth-rate "producers" peddle their shoddy wares with the full approval of evangelical leaders who can even quote a holy text in defense of their delinquency. And hardly a man dares raise his voice against it.

The great god Entertainment amuses his devotees mainly by telling them stories. The love of stories, which is a characteristic of childhood, has taken fast hold of the minds of the retarded saints of our day, so much so that not a few persons manage to make a comfortable living by spinning yarns and serving them up in various disguises to church people. What is natural and beautiful in a child may be shocking when it persists into adulthood, and more so when it appears in the sanctuary and seeks to pass for true religion.

Is it not a strange thing and a wonder that, with the shadow of atomic destruction hanging over the world and with the coming of Christ drawing near, the professed followers of the Lord should be giving themselves up to religious amusements? That in an hour when mature saints are so desperately needed vast numbers of believers should revert to spiritual childhood and clamor for religious toys?

"*Remember, O Lord, what is come upon us: consider, and behold our reproach. . . . The crown is fallen from our head: woe unto us, that we have sinned! For this our heart is faint; for these things our eyes are dim.*" AMEN. AMEN.

Bible Taught or Spirit Taught?

It may shock some readers to suggest that there is a difference between being Bible taught and being Spirit taught. Nevertheless it is so.

It is altogether possible to be instructed in the rudiments of the faith and still have no real understanding of the whole thing. And it is possible to go on to become expert in Bible doctrine and not have spiritual illumination, with the result that a veil remains over the mind, preventing it from apprehending the truth in its spiritual essence.

Most of us are acquainted with churches that teach the Bible to their children from their tenderest years, give them long instruction in the catechism, drill them further in pastor's classes, and still never produce in them a living Christianity nor a virile godliness. Their members show no evidence of having passed from death unto life. None of the earmarks of salvation so plainly indicated in the Scriptures are found among them. Their religious lives are correct and reasonably moral, but wholly mechanical and altogether lacking in radiance. They wear their faith as persons in mourning once wore black arm bands to show their love and respect for the departed.

Such persons cannot be dismissed as hypocrites. Many of them are pathetically serious about it all. They are simply blind. From lack of the vital Spirit they are forced to get along with the outward shell of faith, while all the time their deep hearts are starving for spiritual reality and they do not know what is wrong with them.

This difference between the religion of creed and the religion of the Spirit is well set forth by the saintly Thomas in a tender little prayer to his Lord: "The children of Israel in time past said unto Moses, 'Speak thou with us, and we will hear: but let not God speak with us, lest we die.' Not so, Lord, not so, I beseech Thee; but rather with the prophet Samuel, I humbly and earnestly entreat, 'Speak, Lord; for thy servant heareth.' Let not Moses speak unto me, nor any of the prophets, but rather do Thou speak, O Lord God, the inspirer, enlightener of all the prophets; for Thou alone without them canst perfectly instruct me, but they without Thee can profit nothing. They indeed may utter words, but they cannot give the Spirit. Most beautifully do they speak, but if Thou be silent, they inflame not the heart. They teach the letter, but Thou openest the sense; they bring forth mysteries, but Thou unlockest the meaning of sealed things. . . . They work only outwardly, but Thou instructest and enlightenest the heart. . . . They cry aloud with words, but Thou impartest understanding to the hearing."

It would be hard to wrap it up better than that. The same thing has been said variously by others; however, the most familiar saying probably is, "The Scriptures, to be understood, must be read with the same Spirit that originally inspired them." No one denies this, but even such a statement will go over the heads of those who hear it unless the Holy Spirit inflames the heart.

The charge often made against us by Liberals, that we are "bibliolaters," is probably not true in the same sense as meant by our detractors; but candor and self-analysis will force us to admit that there is often too much truth in their charge. Among religious persons of unquestioned orthodoxy there is sometimes found a dull dependence upon the letter of the text without the faintest understanding of its spirit. That truth is in its essence spiritual must constantly be kept before our minds if we would know the truth indeed. Jesus Christ is Himself the Truth, and He cannot be confined to mere words even though, as we ardently believe, He has Himself inspired the words. That which is spiritual cannot be shut in by ink or fenced in by type and paper. The best a book can do is to give us the letter of truth. If we ever receive more than this, it must be by the Holy Spirit who gives it.

The great need of the hour among persons spiritually hungry is twofold: First, to know the Scriptures, apart from which no saving truth will be vouchsafed by our Lord; the second, to be enlightened by the Spirit, apart from whom the Scriptures will not be understood.

The Terror of the Lord

A truth fully taught in the Scriptures and verified in personal experience by countless numbers of holy men and women through the centuries might be condensed thus into a religious axiom: *No one can know the true grace of God who has not first known the fear of God.*

The first announcement of God's redemptive intention toward mankind was made to a man and a woman hiding in mortal fear from the presence of the Lord. The Law of God was given to a man trembling in terror amid fire and smoke, and quaking at the voice of thunder and the sound of the divine trumpet. When Zacharias' tongue was loosened by the mysterious operation of God "fear came on all that dwelt round about." Even the famous annunciation, "On earth peace, good will toward men," was given to shepherds who were "sore afraid" by reason of the sudden overwhelming presence of the heavenly host.

We have but to read the Scriptures with our eyes open and we can see this truth running like a strong cable from Genesis to Revelation. The presence of the divine always brought fear to the hearts of sinful men. Always there was about any manifestation of God something that dismayed the onlookers, that daunted and overawed them, that struck them with a terror more than natural. This terror had no relation to mere fear of bodily harm. It was a dread consternation experienced far in toward the center and core of the nature, much farther in than that fear experienced as a normal result of the instinct for physical self-preservation.

I do not believe that any lasting good can come from religious activities that do not root in this quality of creature-fear. The animal in us is very strong and altogether self-confident. Until it has been defeated God will not show Himself to the eyes of our faith. Until we have been gripped by that nameless terror which results when an unholy creature is suddenly confronted by that One who is the holiest of all, we are not likely to be much affected by the doctrine of love and grace as it is declared by the New Testament evangel. The love of God affects a carnal heart not at all; or if at all, then adversely, for the knowledge that God loves us may simply confirm us in our self-righteousness.

The effort of liberal and borderline modernists to woo men to God by presenting the soft side of religion is an unqualified evil because it ignores the very reason for our alienation from God in the first place. Until a man has gotten into trouble with his heart he is not likely to get out of trouble with God. Cain and Abel are two solemn examples of this truth. Cain brought a present to One whom he assumed to be pleased with him. Abel brought a sacrifice to One who he knew could not accept him as he was. His trembling heart told him to find a place to hide. Cain's heart did not tremble. Cain was well satisfied with himself, so he sought no hiding place. The fear of God would have served Cain well in that critical moment, for it would have changed the whole character of his offering and altered the entire course of his life for the better.

As indispensable as is the terror of the Lord, we must always keep in mind that it cannot be induced by threats made in the name of the Lord. Hell and judgment are realities, and they must be preached in their Biblical context as fully as the Bible teaches them, no more and no less; but they cannot induce that mysterious thing we call the fear of the Lord. Such fear is a supernatural thing, having no relation to threats of punishment. It has about it a mysterious quality, often without much intellectual content; it is a *feeling* rather than an idea; it is the deep reaction of a fallen creature in the presence of the holy Being the stunned heart knows is God. The Holy Spirit alone can induce this emotion in the human breast. All effort on our part to superinduce it is wasted, or worse.

Because the fear of God is a supernatural thing

it can never be raised by repeated warnings about war or Communism or depressions. The current trick of frightening people into accepting Christ by threatening them with atom bombs and guided missiles is not scriptural, neither is it effective. By shooting off firecrackers in the face of a flock of goats you could conceivably succeed in herding them into a sheepfold; but all the natural fear in the world cannot make a sheep out of a goat. And neither can fear of a Russian invasion turn impenitent men into lovers of God and righteousness. It just does not work that way.

Whence then does the true fear of God arise? From the knowledge of our own sinfulness and a sense of the presence of God. Isaiah had an acute experience both of his personal uncleanness and of the awesome presence of Jehovah: the two were more than he could stand. On his face he cried out a confession of his own sinfulness, made all the more intolerable because his eyes had seen the King, even the Lord of Hosts.

A congregation will feel this mysterious terror of God when the minister and the leaders of the church are filled with the Spirit. When Moses came down from the mount with his face shining the children of Israel were afraid with a fear born out of that supernatural sight. Moses did not need to threaten them. He had only to appear before them with that light on his face.

No Regeneration Without Reformation

In the Bible the offer of pardon on the part of God is conditioned upon intention to reform on the part of man. There can be no spiritual regeneration till there has been a moral reformation. That this statement requires defense only proves how far from the truth we have strayed.

In our current popular theology pardon depends upon faith alone. The very word *reform* has been banished from among the sons of the Reformation!

We often hear the declaration, "I do not preach reformation; I preach regeneration." Now we recognize this as being the expression of a commendable revolt against the insipid and unscriptural doctrine of salvation by human effort. But the declaration as it stands contains real error, for it opposes reformation to regeneration. Actually the two are never opposed to each other in sound Bible theology. The not-reformation-but-regeneration doctrine incorrectly presents us with an either-or; either you take reformation or you take regeneration. This is inaccurate. The fact is that on this subject we are presented not with an either-or, but with a both-and. The converted man is both reformed and regenerated. And unless the sinner is willing to reform his way of living he will never know the inward experience of regeneration. This is the vital truth which has gotten lost under the leaves in popular evangelical theology.

The idea that God will pardon a rebel who has not given up his rebellion is contrary both to the Scriptures and to common sense. How horrible to contemplate a church full of persons who have been pardoned but who still love sin and hate the ways of righteousness. And how much more horrible to think of heaven as filled with sinners who had not repented nor changed their way of living.

A familiar story will illustrate this. The governor of one of our states was visiting the state prison incognito. He fell into conversation with a personable young convict and felt a secret wish to pardon him. "What would you do," he asked casually, "if you were lucky enough to obtain a pardon?" The convict, not knowing to whom he was speaking, snarled his reply: "If I ever get out of this place, the first thing I'll do is to cut the throat of the judge who sent me here." The governor broke off the conversation and withdrew from the cell. The convict stayed on in prison. To pardon a man who had not reformed would be to let loose another killer upon society. That kind of pardon would not only be foolish, it would be downright immoral.

The promise of pardon and cleansing is always associated in the Scriptures with the command to repent. The widely-used text in Isaiah, "Though your sins be as scarlet, they shall be as white as snow; though they be red like crimson, they shall be as wool," is organically united to the verses that precede it: "Wash you, make you clean; put away the evil of your doings from before mine eyes; cease to do evil; learn to do well; seek judgment, relieve the oppressed, judge the fatherless, plead for the widow." What does this teach but radical reformation of life before there can be any expectation of pardon? To divorce the words from each other is to do violence to the Scriptures and to convict ourselves of deceitfully handling the truth.

I think there is little doubt that the teaching of salvation without repentance has lowered the moral standards of the Church and produced a multitude of deceived religious professors who erroneously believe themselves to be saved when in fact they are still in the gall of bitterness and the bond of iniquity. And to see such persons actually seeking the deeper life is a grim and disillusioning sight. Yet our altars are sometimes filled with seekers who are crying with Simon, "Give me this power," when the moral groundwork has simply not been laid for it. The whole thing must be acknowledged as a clear victory for the devil, a victory he could never have enjoyed if unwise teachers had not made it possible by preaching the evil doctrine of regeneration apart from reformation.

Faith Is a Perturbing Thing

"Faith," said the early Lutherans, "is a perturbing thing."

To Martin Luther goes the credit under God for having rediscovered the Biblical doctrine of justification by faith. Luther's emphasis upon faith as the only way into peace of heart and deliverance from sin gave a new impulse of life to the decadent Church and brought about the Reformation. That much is history. It is not a matter of opinion but of simple fact. Anyone can check it.

But something has happened to the doctrine of justification by faith as Luther taught it. What has happened is not so easily discovered. It is not a matter of simple fact, a plain yes or no, an obvious black or white. It is more elusive than that, and very much more difficult to come at; but what has happened is so serious and so vital that it has changed or is in the process of changing the whole evangelical outlook. If it continues it may well turn Christianity inside out and put for the faith of our fathers something else entirely. And the whole spiritual revolution will be so gradual and so innocent appearing that it will hardly be noticed. Anyone who fights it will be accused of jousting against windmills like Don Quixote.

The faith of Paul and Luther was a revolutionizing thing. It upset the whole life of the individual and made him into another person altogether. It laid hold on the life and brought it under obedience to Christ. It took up its cross and followed along after Jesus with no intention of going back. It said goodbye to its old friends as certainly as Elijah when he stepped into the fiery chariot and went away in the whirlwind. It had a finality about it. It snapped shut on a man's heart like a trap; it captured the man and made him from that moment forward a happy loveservant of his Lord. It turned earth into a desert and drew heaven within sight of the believing soul. It realigned all life's actions and brought them into accord with the will of God. It set its possessor on a pinnacle of truth from which spiritual vantage point he viewed everything that came into his field of experience. It made him little and God big and Christ unspeakably dear. All this and more happened to a man when he received the faith that justifies.

Came the revolution, quietly, certainly, and put another construction upon the word "faith." Little by little the whole meaning of the word shifted from what it had been to what it is now. And so insidious was the change that hardly a voice has been raised to warn against it. But the tragic consequences are all around us.

Faith now means no more than passive moral acquiescence in the Word of God and the cross of Jesus. To exercise it we have only to rest on one knee and nod our heads in agreement with the instructions of a personal worker intent upon saving our soul. The general effect is much the same as that which men feel after a visit to a good and wise doctor. They come back from such a visit feeling extra good, withal smiling just a little sheepishly to think how many fears they had entertained about their health when actually there was nothing wrong with them. They just needed a rest.

Such a faith as this does not perturb people. It comforts them. It does not put their hip out of joint so that they halt upon their thigh; rather it teaches them deep breathing exercises and improves their posture. The face of their ego is washed and their self-confidence is rescued from discouragement. All this they gain, but they do not get a new name as Jacob did, nor do they limp into the eternal sunlight. "As he passed over Penuel the sun rose upon him." That was Jacob—rather, that was Israel, for the sun did not shine much upon Jacob. It was ashamed to. But it loved to rest upon the head of the man whom God had transformed.

This generation of Christians must hear again the doctrine of the perturbing quality of faith. People must be told that the Christian religion is not something they can trifle with. The faith of Christ will command or it will have nothing to do with a man. It will not yield to experimentation. Its power cannot reach any man who is secretly keeping an escape route open in case things get too tough for him. The only man who can be sure he has true Bible faith is the one who has put himself in a position where he cannot go back. His faith has resulted in an everlasting and irrevocable committal, and however strongly he may be tempted he always replies, "Lord, to whom shall we go? thou hast the words of eternal life."

True Faith Brings Committal

To many Christians Christ is little more than an idea, or at best an ideal; He is not a fact. Millions of professed believers talk as if He were real and act as if He were not. And always our actual position is to be discovered by the way we act, not by the way we talk.

We can prove our faith by our committal to it, and in no other way. Any belief that does not command the one who holds it is not a real belief; it is a pseudo belief only. And it might shock some of us profoundly if we were brought suddenly face to face with our beliefs and forced to test them in the fires of practical living.

Many of us Christians have become extremely skillful in arranging our lives so as to admit the truth of Christianity without being embarrassed by its implications. We arrange things so that we can get on well enough without divine aid, while at the same time ostensibly seeking it. We boast in the Lord but watch carefully that we never get caught depending on Him. "The heart is deceitful above all things, and desperately wicked: who can know it?"

Pseudo faith always arranges a way out to serve in case God fails it. Real faith knows only one way and gladly allows itself to be stripped of any second way or makeshift substitutes. For true faith, it is either God or total collapse. And not since Adam first stood up on the earth has God failed a single man or woman who trusted Him.

The man of pseudo faith will fight for his verbal creed but refuse flatly to allow himself to get into a predicament where his future must depend upon that creed being true. He always provides himself with secondary ways of escape so he will have a way out if the roof caves in.

What we need very badly these days is a company of Christians who are prepared to trust God as completely now as they know they must do at the last day. For each of us the time is surely coming when we shall have nothing but God. Health and wealth and friends and hiding places will all be swept away and we shall have only God. To the man of pseudo faith that is a terrifying thought, but to real faith it is one of the most comforting thoughts the heart can entertain.

It would be a tragedy indeed to come to the place where we have no other but God and find that we had not really been trusting God during the days of our earthly sojourn. It would be better to invite God now to remove every false trust, to disengage our hearts from all secret hiding places and to bring us out into the open where we can discover for ourselves whether or not we actually trust Him. That is a harsh cure for our troubles, but it is a sure one. Gentler cures may be too weak to do the work. And time is running out on us.

The Great Disparity

There is an evil which I have seen under the sun and which in its effect upon the Christian religion may be more destructive than Communism, Romanism and Liberalism combined. It is the glaring disparity between theology and practice among professing Christians.

So wide is the gulf that separates theory from practice in the church that an inquiring stranger who chances upon both would scarcely dream that there was any relation between them. An intelligent observer of our human scene who heard the Sunday morning sermon and later watched the Sunday afternoon conduct of those who had heard it would

51

conclude that he had been examining two distinct and contrary religions.

A church conference, for instance, may listen to and applaud the most spiritual message, and twenty minutes later adopt the most carnal procedure, altogether as if they had not heard the impassioned moral appeal a few moments before. Christians habitually weep and pray over beautiful truth, only to draw back from that same truth when it comes to the difficult job of putting it in practice. The average church simply does not dare to check its practices against Biblical precepts. It tolerates things that are diametrically opposed to the will of God, and if the matter is pointed out to its leaders they will defend its unscriptural practices with a smooth casuistry equal to the verbal dodging of the Roman moralists.

This can be explained only by assuming a lack of integration in the religious personality. There seems to be no vital connection between the emotional and volitional departments of the life. The mind can approve and the emotions enjoy while the will drags its feet and refuses to go along. And since Christ makes His appeal directly to the will, are we not justified in wondering whether or not these divided souls have ever made a true committal to the Lord? Or whether they have been inwardly renewed?

It appears that too many Christians want to enjoy the thrill of feeling right but are not willing to endure the inconvenience of being right. So the divorce between theory and practice becomes permanent in fact, though in word the union is declared to be eternal. Truth sits forsaken and grieves till her professed followers come home for a brief visit, but she sees them depart again when the bills become due. They protest great and undying love for her but they will not let their love cost them anything.

Could this be the condition our Lord had in mind when He said, "Thou hast a name that thou livest, and art dead"? What can the effect be upon the spectators who live day after day among professed Christians who habitually ignore the commandments of Christ and live after their own private notions of Christianity? Will they not conclude that the whole thing is false? Will they not be forced to believe that the faith of Christ is an unreal and visionary thing which they are fully justified in rejecting?

Certainly the non-Christian is not too much to be blamed if he turns disgustedly away from the invitation of the Gospel after he has been exposed for a while to the inconsistencies of those of his acquaintance who profess to follow Christ. The deadening effect of religious make-believe on the human mind is beyond all describing.

In that great and terrible day when the deeds of men are searched into by the penetrating eyes of the Judge of all the earth what will we answer when we are charged with inconsistency and moral fraud? And at whose door will lie the blame for the millions of lost men who while they lived on earth were sickened and revolted by the religious travesty they knew as Christianity?

Our Enemy Contentment

One of the big milk companies makes capital of the fact that their cows are all satisfied with their lot in life. Their clever ads have made the term "contented cows" familiar to everyone. But what is a virtue in a cow may be a vice in a man. And contentment, when it touches spiritual things, is surely a vice.

Paul professed that he had learned to be content with such earthly goods as fell to his lot. That is something else from being content with his spiritual attainments. With these he specifically declared that he was not satisfied: "Brethren, I count not myself to have apprehended: but this one thing I do, forgetting those things which are behind, and reaching forth unto those things which are before, I press toward the mark for the prize of the high calling of God in Christ Jesus." Contentment with earthly goods is the mark of a saint; contentment with our spiritual state is a mark of inward blindness.

One of the greatest foes of the Christian is religious complacency. The man who believes he has arrived will not go any farther; from his standpoint it would be foolish to do so. The snare is to believe we have arrived when we have not. The present neat habit of quoting a text to prove we have arrived may be a dangerous one if in truth we have no actual inward experience of the text. Truth that is not experienced is no better than error, and may be fully as dangerous. The scribes who sat in Moses' seat were not the victims of error; they were the victims of their failure to experience the truth they taught.

Religious complacency is encountered almost everywhere among Christians these days, and its presence is a sign and a prophecy. For every Christian will become at last what his desires have made him. We are all the sum total of our hungers. The great saints have all had thirsting hearts. Their cry has been, "My soul thirsteth for God, for the living God: when shall I come and appear before God?" Their longing after God all but consumed them; it propelled them onward and upward to heights toward which less ardent Christians look with languid eye and entertain no hope of reaching.

Orthodox Christianity has fallen to its present low estate from lack of spiritual desire. Among the many who profess the Christian faith scarcely one in a thousand reveals any passionate thirst for God. The practice of many of our spiritual advisers is to use the Scriptures to discourage such little longings as may be discovered here and there among us. We fear extremes and shy away from too much ardor in religion as if it were possible to have too much love or too much faith or too much holiness.

Occasionally one's heart is cheered by the discovery of some insatiable saint who is willing to sacrifice everything for the sheer joy of experiencing God in increasing intimacy. To such we offer this word of exhortation: Pray on, fight on, sing on. Do not underrate anything God may have done for you heretofore. Thank God for everything up to this point, but do not stop here. Press on into the deep things of God. Insist upon tasting the profounder mysteries of redemption. Keep your feet on the ground, but let your heart soar as high as it will. Refuse to be average or to surrender to the chill of your spiritual environment. If you thus "follow after," heaven will surely be opened to you and you will, with Ezekiel, see visions of God.

Unless you do these things you will reach at last (and unknown to you) the bone yard of orthodoxy and be doomed to live out your days in a spiritual state which can be best described as "the dead level and quintessence of every mediocrity. "

From such a state God save us all. AMEN.

Christ Is the Pattern

Religion correctly assumes the fluidity of human nature. It assumes that the human character is in flux and can be directed into prechosen channels leading to desired ends.

Could human nature be shown to be static, religion would instantly lose most of its meaning. For the one thing that religious persons want most is to be changed, to be made over from what they are into something they desire to be.

The Christian faith takes for granted that men should be and can be changed, and the change it sets before them is so radical as to amount to a moral transformation. The message of Christ lays hold upon a man with the intention to alter him, to mold him again after another image and make of him something altogether different from what he had been before.

"Be ye transformed by the renewing of your mind" is the injunction laid upon believing men by the apostle.

Now, granted that men may be changed and that the power of God in the Gospel can change them, the important question naturally is, Into what image are they to be changed? Who or what is to be the model for them?

To this question there have been many answers given. The quasi-Christian religious philosophy so popular today answers that there is a "norm" somewhere in human nature from which we have departed to a greater or lesser degree and to which we must be restored. So religion is brought in to aid in the restoration. It operates by "adjusting" the inquiring soul, first to himself and then to society. Everything depends upon this work of adjustment. Human nature, so runs the theory, is basically right and good, but it has been put out of focus by the world stresses in which it is compelled to live. It has been warped by environment, by bad teaching and by various harmful influences, beginning at the time of its birth or before.

The whole burden of this type of religious thinking is to restore the man to an image of himself. All he needs is to be made into his own likeness again, to become "a real person," free from the warping influences of prejudice, fear and superstition. He was all right to begin with, as were his ancestors before him, and his highest present goal is to be restored, like a damaged painting, so that the hand of the master may again be discovered under the soil and grime of life.

All this sounds just cozy, but the trouble is that the underlying idea is completely false, and all the religious hopes and dreams arising from it are and must be without foundation.

The message of the New Testament is bluntly opposite to this. People are *not* all right except for minor maladjustments. They are lost, inwardly lost, morally and spiritually lost. That has been the persistent Christian testimony from the first, and human history has shown how correct it is. There is nothing in us that can serve as a model for the new man. Conformity to ourselves, even our better selves, can lead only to ultimate tragedy. The human heart is deceitful above all things and desperately wicked. It must have help from outside itself, from above itself, if it is to escape the gravitational pull of its own sinful nature. And this help the Gospel furnishes in full and sufficient measure.

The Gospel not only furnishes transforming power to remold the human heart; it provides also a model after which the new life is to be fashioned, and that model is Christ Himself. Christ is God acting like God in the lowly raiments of human flesh. Yet He is also man; so He becomes the perfect model after which redeemed human nature is to be fashioned.

The beginnings of that transformation which is to change the believing man's nature from the image of sin to the image of God are found in conversion when the man is made a partaker of the divine nature. By regeneration and sanctification, by faith and prayer, by suffering and discipline, by the Word and the Spirit, the work goes on till the dream of God has been realized in the Christian heart. Everything that God does in His ransomed children has as its long-range purpose the final restoration of the divine image in human nature. Everything looks forward to the consummation.

In the meantime the Christian himself can work along with God in bringing about the great change. Paul tells us how: "But we all, with open face beholding as in a glass the glory of the Lord, are changed into the same image from glory to glory even as by the Spirit of the Lord" (2 Cor. 3:18).

The Cross Is a Radical Thing

The cross of Christ is the most revolutionary thing ever to appear among men.

The cross of old Roman times knew no compromise; it never made concessions. It won all its arguments by killing its opponent and silencing him for good. It spared not Christ, but slew Him the same as the rest. He was alive when they hung Him on that cross and completely dead when they took Him down six hours later. That was the cross the first time it appeared in Christian history.

After Christ was risen from the dead the apostles went out to preach His message, and what they preached was the cross. And wherever they went into the wide world they carried the cross, and the same revolutionary power went with them. The radical message of the cross transformed Saul of Tarsus and changed him from a persecutor of Christians to a tender believer and an apostle of the faith. Its power changed bad men into good ones. It shook off the long bondage of paganism and altered completely the whole moral and mental outlook of the Western world.

All this it did and continued to do as long as it was permitted to remain what it had been originally, a cross. Its power departed when it was changed from a thing of death to a thing of beauty. When men made of it a symbol, hung it around their necks as an ornament or made its outline before their faces as a magic sign to ward off evil, then it became at best a weak emblem, at worst a positive fetish. As such it is revered today by millions who know absolutely nothing about its power.

The cross effects its ends by destroying one established pattern, the victim's, and creating another pattern, its own. Thus it always has its way. It wins by defeating its opponent and imposing its will upon him. It always dominates. It never compromises, never dickers nor confers, never surrenders a point for the sake of peace. It cares not for peace; it cares only to end its opposition as fast as possible.

With perfect knowledge of all this Christ said, "If any man will come after me, let him deny himself, and take up his cross, and follow me." So the cross not only brings Christ's life to an end, it ends also the first life, the old life, of every one of His true followers. It destroys the old pattern, the Adam pattern, in the believer's life, and brings it to an end. Then the God who raised Christ from the dead raises the believer and a new life begins.

This, and nothing less, is true Christianity, though

we cannot but recognize the sharp divergence of this conception from that held by the rank and file of evangelicals today. But we dare not qualify our position. The cross stands high above the opinions of men and to that cross all opinions must come at last for judgment. A shallow and worldly leadership would modify the cross to please the entertainment-mad saintlings who will have their fun even within the very sanctuary; but to do so is to court spiritual disaster and risk the anger of the Lamb turned Lion.

We must do something about the cross, and one of two things only we can do—flee it or die upon it. And if we should be so foolhardy as to flee we shall by that act put away the faith of our fathers and make of Christianity something other than it is. Then we shall have left only the empty language of salvation; the power will depart with our departure from the true cross.

If we are wise we will do what Jesus did: endure the cross and despise its shame for the joy that is set before us. To do this is to submit the whole pattern of our lives to be destroyed and built again in the power of an endless life. And we shall find that it is more than poetry, more than sweet hymnody and elevated feeling. The cross will cut into our lives where it hurts worst, sparing neither us nor our carefully cultivated reputations. It will defeat us and bring our selfish lives to an end. Only then can we rise in fullness of life to establish a pattern of living wholly new and free and full of good works.

The changed attitude toward the cross that we see in modern orthodoxy proves not that God has changed, nor that Christ has eased up on His demand that we carry the cross; it means rather that current Christianity has moved away from the standards of the New Testament. So far have we moved indeed that it may take nothing short of a new reformation to restore the cross to its right place in the theology and life of the Church.

We Must Die If We Would Live

"Let me die—lest I die—only let me see Thy face." That was the prayer of St. Augustine.

"Hide not Thy face from me," he cried in an agony of desire. "Oh! that I might repose on Thee. Oh! that Thou wouldst enter into my heart, and inebriate it, that I may forget my ills, and embrace Thee, my sole good."

This longing to die, to get our opaque form out

of the way so that it might not hide from us the lovely face of God, is one that is instantly understood by the hungry-hearted believer. To die that we might not die! There is no contradiction here, for there are before us two kinds of dying, a dying to be sought and a dying to be avoided at any cost.

To Augustine the sight of God inwardly enjoyed was life itself and anything less than that was death. To exist in total eclipse under the shadow of nature without the realized Presence was a condition not to be tolerated. Whatever hid God's face from him must be taken out of the way, even his own self-love, his dearest ego, his most cherished treasures. So he prayed, "Let me die."

The great saint's daring prayer was heard and, as might be expected, was answered with a fullness of generosity characteristic of God. He died the kind of death to which Paul testified: "I am crucified with Christ: nevertheless I live; yet not I, but Christ liveth in me." His life and ministry continued and his presence is always there, in his books, in the church, in history; but wondrous as it may be, he is strangely transparent; his own personality is scarcely seen, while the light of Christ shines through with a kind of healing splendor.

There have been those who have thought that to get themselves out of the way it was necessary to withdraw from society; so they denied all natural human relationships and went into the desert or the mountain or the hermit's cell to fast and labor and struggle to mortify their flesh. While their motive was good it is impossible to commend their method. For it is not scriptural to believe that the old Adam nature can be conquered in that manner. It is altogether too tough to be killed by abusing the body or starving the affections. It yields to nothing less than the cross.

In every Christian's heart there is a cross and a throne, and the Christian is on the throne till he puts himself on the cross; if he refuses the cross he remains on the throne. Perhaps this is at the bottom of the backsliding and worldliness among gospel believers today. We want to be saved but we insist that Christ do all the dying. No cross for us, no dethronement, no dying. We remain king within the little kingdom of Mansoul and wear our tinsel crown with all the pride of a Caesar; but we doom ourselves to shadows and weakness and spiritual sterility.

If we will not die then we must die, and that death will mean the forfeiture of many of those everlasting treasures which the saints have cherished. Our uncrucified flesh will rob us of purity of heart, Christlikeness of character, spiritual insight, fruitfulness; and more than all, it will hide from us the vision of God's face, that vision which has been the light of earth and will be the completeness of heaven.

Christ Died for Our Hearts

The human heart lives by its sympathies and affections. In the day that will try every man's works how much we know will not come in for much consideration. What and whom we have loved will be about all that matters then. For this reason we can never give too great care to the condition of our inner lives.

The vital place of the moral sympathies in human character has not in recent times received from our religious teachers the attention it deserves. We are only now emerging from a long ice age during which an undue emphasis was laid upon objective truth at the expense of subjective experience. The climate in evangelical circles was definitely chilly. We made the serious mistake of taking each other as criteria against which to judge our spiritual lives instead of comparing notes with Bible saints and with the superior lovers of God whose devotional works and inspired hymns linger like a holy fragrance long after they themselves have left this earthly scene.

The reason back of this huge error is not hard

to discover. The movement toward objective truth and away from religious emotion was in reality a retreat from fanaticism. Bible-loving Christians half a century ago were repulsed by certain gross manifestations of religious flesh on the part of some of the very ones who laid claim to the most exalted spiritual experiences, and as a result fled from wild fire to deep freeze. Bible teachers became afraid to admit the validity of the religious sympathies. The text became the test of orthodoxy, and Fundamentalism, the most influential school of evangelical Christianity, went over to textualism. The inner life was neglected in a constant preoccupation with the "truth," and truth was interpreted to mean doctrinal truth only. No other meaning of the word was allowed. Objectivism had won. The human heart cowered in its cold cellar, ashamed to show its face.

As might have been foreseen, this resulted in a steady decline in the quality of Christian worship on the one hand and, on the other, the rise of religious entertainment as a source of mental pleasure. Wise leaders should have known that the human heart cannot exist in a vacuum. If men do not have joy in their hearts they will seek it somewhere else. If Christians are forbidden to enjoy the wine of the Spirit they will turn to the wine of the flesh for enjoyment. And that is exactly what fundamental Christianity (as well as the so-called "full gospel" groups) has done in the last quarter century. God's people have turned to the amusements of the world to try to squeeze a bit of juice out of them for the relief of their dry and joyless hearts. "Gospel" boogie singing now furnishes for many persons the only religious joy they know. Others wipe their eyes tenderly over "gospel" movies, and a countless number of amusements flourish everywhere, paid for by the consecrated tithes of persons who ought to know better. Our teachers took away our right to be happy in God and the human heart wreaked its terrible vengeance by going on a fleshly binge from which the evangelical Church will not soon recover, if indeed it ever does. For multitudes of professed Christians today the Holy Spirit is not a necessity. They have learned to cheer their hearts and warm their hands at other fires. And scores of publishers and various grades of "producers" are waxing fat on their delinquency.

The human heart with its divine capacity for holy pleasure must no longer be allowed to remain the victim of fear and bad teaching. Christ died for our hearts and the Holy Spirit wants to come and satisfy them.

Let us emulate Isaac and open again the wells our fathers digged and which have been stopped up by the enemy. The waters are there, cool, sweet and satisfying. They will spring up again at the touch of the honest spade. Who will start digging?

We Stand in Christ's Triumph

Among evangelicals it is a commonplace to say that the superiority of Christianity to every other religion lies in the fact that in Christianity a *Person* is present, active, filling, upholding and supporting all. That Person, of course, is Jesus Christ.

That is what we say, and say truthfully, but my own experience has shown how difficult it is to make this belief a practical force in my own life. And a little observation reveals that my fellow evangelicals for the most part are not doing much better. This mighty world-beating truth gets lost under a multitude of lesser truths and is allowed to lie forgotten while we struggle, mostly unsuccessfully, with the world, the flesh and the devil.

The unique thing about the early Christians was their radiant relation to a Person. "The Lord," they called Him tenderly, and when they used the term they gave it its own New Testament meaning. It meant Jesus Christ who a short while before had been among them but was now gone into the heavens as their High Priest and Advocate.

It was this engrossment with a victorious Person that gave verve and vibrancy to their lives and conviction to their testimony. They bore witness joyously to the One who had lived as a true Man among men. Their testimony was not weakened by the pale cast of metaphysical thought. They knew that Jesus was very Man and very God, and He had died, had been raised from the dead and had ascended into heaven. They accepted literally His claim to be invested with authority over everything in heaven, earth and hell. How it could be they never stopped to inquire. They trusted Him absolutely and left the details to their triumphant Lord.

Another marked characteristic of the witness of those first Christians was their insistence that Jesus was Lord and mover in a long-range plan to restore the earth and to bring it again under divine control. He is now sovereign Head of His body the Church, they declared, and will extend His rule to include the earth and the world in His own good time. Hence they never presented Him as Saviour merely. It never occured to them to invite people to receive "peace of mind" or "peace of soul." Nor did they stop at forgiveness or joy or happiness. They gathered up all these benefits into one Person and preached that Person as the last and highest sum of every good possible to be known and enjoyed in this world or that which is to come. "The same Lord over all," they said, "is rich unto all that call upon him." The seeker must own Him Lord triumphant, not a meek-eyed Lover of their souls only, but Lord above all question or doubt.

Today we hold the same views, but our *emphasis* is not the same. The meek and lowly Jesus has displaced the high and holy Jesus in the minds of millions. The vibrant note of triumph is missing in our witness. A sad weeping Jesus offers us His quiet sympathy in our griefs and temptations, but He appears to be as helpless as we are when the pressure is on. His pale feminine face looks at us from the "holy picture" of the Catholic and the Easter card of the Protestant. We give Him our sympathy, but scarcely our confidence. The helpless Christ of the crucifix and the vacuous-countenanced Christ that looks out in sweet innocence from the walls of our evangelical homes is all one and the same. The Catholics rescue Him by bringing a Queen of Heaven to His aid. But we Protestants have no helper. So we sing pop choruses to cheer our drooping spirits and hold panel discussions in the plaintive hope that someone will come up with the answer to our scarce-spoken complaint.

Well, we already have the answer if we but had the faith and wisdom to turn to it. The answer is Christ Victorious, high over all. He lives forever above the reach of His foes. He has but to speak and it is done; He need but command and heaven and earth obey Him. Within the broad framework of His far-looking plans He tolerates for a time the wild outlawry of a fallen world, but He holds the earth in His hand and can call the nation to judgment whenever He wills.

Yes, Christian pilgrim, we are better off than the sad Church can see. We stand in Christ's triumph. Because He lives we live also. *Thanks be to God which giveth us the victory through our Lord Jesus Christ.*

To Be or To Do

Historically the West has tended to throw its chief emphasis upon doing and the East upon being. What we *are* has always seemed more important to the Oriental; the Occidental has been willing to settle for what we *do*. One has glorified the verb *to be;* the other, the verb *to do*.

Were human nature perfect there would be no discrepancy between being and doing. The unfallen man would simply live from within, without giving it a thought. His actions would be the true expression of his inner being.

With human nature what it is, however, things are not so simple. Sin has introduced moral confusion and life has become involved and difficult. Those elements within us which were meant to work together in unconscious harmony are often isolated from each other wholly or in part and tend to become actually hostile to each other. For this reason symmetry of character is extremely difficult to achieve.

Out of deep inner confusion arises the antagonism between being and doing, and the verb upon which we throw our emphasis puts us in one of the two catagories: we are *be*-ers or we are *do*-ers, one or the other. In our modern civilized society the stress falls almost wholly upon doing.

We Christians cannot escape this question. We must discover where God throws the stress and come around to the divine pattern. And this should not be too difficult since we have before us the sacred Scriptures with all their wealth of spiritual instruction, and to interpret those Scriptures we have the very Spirit which inspired them.

In spite of all our opportunity to know the truth, most of us are still slow to learn. The tendency to accept without question and follow without knowing why is very strong in us. For this reason whatever the majority of Christians hold at any given time is sure to be accepted as true and right beyond a doubt. It is easier to imitate than to originate; it is easier and, for the time being, safer to fall into step without asking too many questions about where the parade is headed.

This is why *being* has ceased to have much appeal for people and *doing* engages almost everyone's attention. Modern Christians lack symmetry. They know almost nothing about the inner life. They are like a temple that is all exterior without any interior. Color, light, sound, appearance, motion—these are thy gods, O Israel.

"The accent in the Church today," says Leonard Ravenhill, the English evangelist, "is not on devotion, but on commotion." Religious extroversion has been carried to such an extreme in evangelical circles that hardly anyone has the desire, to say nothing of the courage, to question the soundness of it. Externalism has taken over. God now speaks by the wind and the earthquake only; the still small voice can be heard no more. The whole religious machine has become a noisemaker. The adolescent taste which loves the loud horn and the thundering exhaust has gotten into the activities of modern Christians. The old question, "What is the chief end of man?" is now answered, "To dash about the world and add to the din thereof." And all this is done in the name of

Him who did not strive nor cry nor make His voice to be heard in the streets (Mat. 12:18-21).

We must begin the needed reform by challenging the spiritual validity of externalism. What a man is must be shown to be more important than what he does. While the moral quality of any act is imparted by the condition of the heart, there may be a world of religious activity which arises not from within but from without and which would seem to have little or no moral content. Such religious conduct is imitative or reflex. It stems from the current cult of commotion and possesses no sound inner life.

The message "Christ in you, the hope of glory," needs to be restored to the Church. We must show a new generation of nervous, almost frantic, Christians that power lies at the center of the life. Speed and noise are evidences of weakness, not strength. Eternity is silent; time is noisy. Our preoccupation with time is sad evidence of our basic want of faith. The desire to be dramatically active is proof of our religious infantilism; it is a type of exhibitionism common to the kindergarten.

Make Room for Mystery

So finely are the lines of truth drawn, so delicately are the scales of wisdom balanced, that it is not a wonder that some tender-minded Christians become confused and adopt a discouraged attitude toward the Word of God.

The beginner in Christ will not have read long in the Scriptures till he comes upon passages that appear to contradict each other. He may check the various versions or, if he is fortunate enough to read the Scriptures in the original languages, he may consult all the lexicons and still be forced to acknowledge the contradiction. As far as he can see it is there and there is no avoiding it. Now what?

Well, he may do one of several things. He may, for instance, quit in despair and conclude that he can never understand the Bible and that there is no use to try; or he may worry over the contradictory passages until he gets himself into a dangerous state of mind; or (and this is the worst of all) he may consult some of the rationalistic-orthodox theologians who in fancied near-omniscience presume to resolve all Biblical difficulties with a wave of their type-writer. This last is sure to be fatal to true spirituality, for the whole heart attitude of these expositors is wrong and they cannot but lead their disciples astray. They belong to that class of persons mentioned by Cicero, who "fear nothing so much as to appear to be in doubt about anything." They proceed on the false assumption that everything in heaven and earth can be explained. And than this nothing could be more glaringly false.

Far better than the attempt to understand is the humility that admits its ignorance and waits quietly on God for His own light to appear in His own time. We will be better able to understand when we have accepted the humbling truth that there are many things in heaven and earth that we shall never be able to understand. It will be good for us to accept the universe and take our place in the mighty web of God's creation, so perfectly known to Him and so slightly known to even the wisest of men. "The meek will he guide in judgment: and the meek will he teach his way."

To those who have (unintentionally) degraded their conception of God to the level of their human understanding it may appear frightening to admit that there are many things in the Scriptures and more things about the Godhead that transcend the human intellect. But a few minutes on our knees looking into the face of Christ will teach us humility, a virtue whose healing qualities have been known by God's elect from time out of mind.

Coleridge gave it as his considered belief that the profoundest sentence ever uttered by human lips was the spontaneous cry of the prophet Ezekiel in the valley of dry bones when asked by the Lord whether those bones could live: "And I answered, O Lord God, thou knowest." Had Ezekiel answered *yes* or *no* he would have closed off his heart to the mighty mystery which confronted him and would have missed the luxury of wonder in the presence of the Majesty on high. For never forget that it is a privilege to wonder, to stand in delighted silence before the Supreme Mystery and whisper, "O Lord God, thou knowest!"

The pitiable attempt of churchmen to explain everything for the smiling unbeliever has had an effect exactly opposite to that which was intended. It has reduced worship to the level of the intellect and introduced the rationalistic spirit into the wonders of religion.

No one should be ashamed to admit that he does not know, and no Christian should fear the effect of such a confession in the realm of things spiritual. Indeed the very power of the cross lies in the fact that it is the wisdom of God and not the wisdom of man. The day we manage to explain everything spiritual will be the day that we have (for ourselves) destroyed everything divine.

Let it be known that in this matter the Christian is definitely not on the defensive. Let the wise of this world insist that we Christians explain our faith and they put into our hand a sword with which we can put them to headlong flight. We have but to turn and ask them to explain *this* world and we shall see how confused they can become. Jesus said on one occasion, "If I have told you earthly things, and ye believe not, how shall ye believe, if I tell you of heavenly things?" If we are compelled to explain, so are they, and we both do a poor job of it, for mystery lies all about us from the atom to the soul of man, and all any of us can do is to bow and say, "O Lord God, thou knowest."

Probably David lying on his back on the green meadow at night, brooding over the mystery of the moon and the stars and the littleness of man in the total scheme of things, worshiping the God who had made him only a little lower than the angels, was a truer man than the astronomer who in his high pride weighs and measures the heavenly bodies. Yet the astronomer need not despair. If he will humble himself and confess his deep inward need, the God of David will teach him how to worship, and by so doing will make him a greater man than he could ever have been otherwise.

The Whole Life Must Pray

Prayer at its best is the expression of the total life.

Certainly there have been and will continue to be instances when an isolated prayer may be answered even when the one uttering it may not have been living an exemplary Christian life. But we assume that most of those who read this page are not satisfied to get a prayer through occasionally; they want to know a more satisfying prayer life, one that elevates and purifies every act of body and mind and integrates the entire personality into a single spiritual unit. Such prayer can only be the result of a life lived in the Spirit.

All things else being equal, our prayers are only as powerful as our lives. In the long pull we pray only as well as we live. Some prayers are like a fire escape, used only in times of critical emergency— never very enjoyable, but used as a way of terrified escape from disaster. They do not represent the regular life of the one who offers them; rather they are the unusual and uncommon acts of the spiritual amateur.

William Law somewhere pleads for Christians to live lives that accord with their prayers, and one of our well-known hymns asks that God help us "to live more nearly as we pray." Most of us in moments of stress have wished that we had lived so that prayer would not be so unnatural to us and have regretted that we had not cultivated prayer to the point where it would be as easy and as natural as breathing.

We do not want to leave the impression that prayer in times of sudden crisis is not a good and a right thing. It most certainly is, and God is said to be a "very present help in trouble"; but no instructed Christian wants to live his whole life on an emergency level. As we go on into God we shall see the excellency of the life of constant communion where all thoughts and acts are prayers, and the entire life becomes one holy sacrifice of praise and worship.

To pray effectively it is required of us that there be no unblessed areas in our lives, no parts of the mind or soul that are not inhabited by the Spirit, no impure desires allowed to live within us, no disparity between our prayers and our conduct.

All this may appear to be placing the standard too high to be reached by men and women under the sun. But it is not so. If Christ is the kind of Saviour He claims to be He should be able to save His people from the bondage of sin. This is not to support the man-made doctrine of "sinless perfection"; it is rather to declare the God-inspired doctrine that it is possible to "walk in the Spirit" and so "not fulfil the lust of the flesh." It is to say that God has made provision in the cross of Christ for His children to be delivered from the galling yoke of sin: "Likewise reckon ye also yourselves to be dead indeed unto sin, but alive unto God through Jesus Christ our Lord."

Undoubtedly the redemption in Christ Jesus has sufficient moral power to enable us to live in a state of purity and love where our whole life will be a prayer. Individual acts of prayer that spring out of that kind of total living will have about them a wondrous power not known to the careless or the worldly Christian.

No Saviourhood Without Lordship

We must never underestimate the ability of human beings to get themselves tangled up.

Mankind appears to have a positive genius for twisting truth until it ceases to be truth and becomes downright falsehood. By overemphasizing in one place and underemphasizing in another the whole pattern of truth may be so altered that a completely false view results without our being aware of it.

This fact was brought forcibly to mind recently by hearing again the discredited doctrine of a divided Christ so widely current a few years ago and still accepted in many religious circles. It goes like this: Christ is both Saviour and Lord. A sinner may be saved by accepting Him as Saviour without yielding to Him as Lord. The practical outworking of this doctrine is that the evangelist presents and the seeker accepts a divided Christ. We have all heard the tearful plea made to persons already saved to accept Christ as Lord and thus enter into the victorious life.

Almost all deeper life teaching is based upon this fallacy, but because it contains a germ of truth its soundness is not questioned. Anyway, it is extremely simple and quite popular, and in addition to these selling points it is also ready-made for both speaker and hearer and requires no thinking by either. So sermons embodying this heresy are freely preached, books are written and songs composed, all saying the same thing; and all saying the wrong thing, except, as I have said, for a feeble germ of truth lying inert at the bottom.

Now, it seems odd that none of these teachers ever noticed that the only true object of saving faith is none other than Christ Himself; not the "saviour-hood" of Christ nor the "lordship" of Christ, but Christ Himself. God does not offer salvation to the one who will believe on one of the offices of Christ, nor is an office of Christ ever presented as an object of faith. Neither are we exhorted to believe on the atonement, nor on the cross, nor on the priesthood of the Saviour. All of these are embodied in the person of Christ, but they are never separated nor is one ever isolated from the rest. Much less are we permitted to accept one of Christ's offices and reject another. The notion that we are so permitted is a modern day heresy, I repeat, and like every heresy it has had evil consequences among Christians. No heresy is ever entertained with impunity. We pay in practical failure for our theoretical errors.

It is altogether doubtful whether any man can be saved who comes to Christ for His help but with no intention to obey Him. Christ's saviourhood is forever united to His lordship. Look at the Scriptures: "If thou shalt confess with thy mouth the Lord Jesus, and shalt believe in thine heart that God hath raised him from the dead, thou shalt be saved . . . for the same Lord over all is rich unto all that call upon him. For whosoever shall call upon the name of the Lord shall be saved" (Rom. 10:9-13). There the *Lord* is the object of faith for salvation. And when the Philippian jailer asked the way to be saved, Paul replied, "Believe on the Lord Jesus Christ, and thou shalt be saved" (Acts 16:31). He did not tell him to believe on the Saviour with the thought that he could later take up the matter of His lordship and settle it at his own convenience. To Paul there could be no division of offices. Christ must be Lord or He will not be Saviour.

There is no intention here to teach that the earnest believer may not go on to explore ever-increasing meanings in Christ, nor do we hold that our first saving contact with Christ brings perfect knowledge of all He is to us. The contrary is true. Ages upon ages will hardly be long enough to allow us to experience all the riches of His grace. As we discover new meanings in His titles and make them ours we will grow in the knowledge of our Lord and in personal appreciation of the multifold offices He fills and the many forms of love He wears exalted on His throne. That is the truth which has been twisted out of shape and reduced to impotence by the doctrine that we can believe on His saviourhood while rejecting His lordship.

"A Sweet Lute, Sweetly Played"

"It is one thing," said Henry Suso, "to hear for oneself a sweet lute, sweetly played, and quite another thing merely to hear about it."

And it is one thing, we may add, to hear truth inwardly for one's very self, and quite another thing merely to hear *about* it.

I do not wish to reflect on the genuineness of any man's religious experience; rather I rejoice in every small shred of true godliness that may yet remain among us in these days of superficiality and pretense. But an examination of the state of things in gospel churches creates a strong suspicion that an alarmingly high percentage of professing Christians today have never heard the lute for themselves. They have only been told about it by others. Their acquaintance with saving truth is by hearsay merely. The mysterious Voice has never penetrated to their own inner ear.

Particularly is this true of the so-called deeper life. Even in those circles where the doctrines of the Spirit-filled life are taken for granted there is a strange lack of inner certainty. We hear the "deeper" truths recited with a glibness that makes us wonder whether the preacher is not telling us about something of which he has only heard, rather than about something which he himself has experienced. The widespread indoctrination in the deeper life without a corresponding enjoyment of the power of the doctrine may easily do more harm than good.

We are turning out from the Bible schools of this country year after year young men and women who know the theory of the Spirit-filled life but do not enjoy the experience. These go out into the churches to create in turn a generation of Christians who have never felt the power of the Spirit and who know nothing personally about the inner fire. The next generation will drop even the theory. That is actually the course some groups have taken over the past years.

One word from the lips of the man who has actually heard the lute play will have more effect than a score of sermons by the man who has only heard that it was played. Acquaintance is always better than hearsay.

How long must we in America go on listening to men who can only tell us what they have read and heard about, never what they themselves have felt and heard and seen?

The All-importance of Motive

The test by which all conduct must finally be judged is motive.

As water cannot rise higher than its source, so the moral quality in an act can never be higher than the motive that inspires it. For this reason no act that arises from an evil motive can be good, even though some good may appear to come out of it. Every deed done out of anger or spite, for instance, will be found at last to have been done for the enemy and against the Kingdom of God.

Unfortunately the nature of religious activity is such that much of it can be carried on for reasons that are not good, such as anger, jealousy, ambition, vanity and avarice. All such activity is essentially evil and will be counted as such at the judgment.

In this matter of motive, as in so many other things, the Pharisees afford us clear examples. They remain the world's most dismal religious failures, not because of doctrinal error nor because they were careless or lukewarm, nor because they were outwardly persons of dissolute life. Their whole trouble lay in the quality of their religious motives. They prayed, but they prayed to be heard of men, and thus their motive ruined their prayers and rendered them not only useless but actually evil. They gave generously to the service of the temple, but they sometimes did it to escape their duty toward their parents, and this was an evil. They judged sin and stood against it when they found it in others, but this they did from self-righteousness and hardness of heart. So with almost everything they did. Their activities had about them an outward appearance of holiness, and those same activities if carried on out of pure motives would have been good and praiseworthy. The whole weakness of the Pharisees lay in the quality of their motives.

That this is not a small matter may be gathered from the fact that those orthodox and proper religionists went on in their blindness till they at last crucified the Lord of glory with no inkling of the gravity of their crime.

Religious acts done out of low motives are twice evil, evil in themselves and evil because they are done in the name of God. This is equivalent to sinning in the name of the sinless One, lying in the name of the One who cannot lie and hating in the name of the One whose nature is love.

Christians, and especially very active ones, should take time out frequently to search their souls to be sure of their motives. Many a solo is sung to show off; many a sermon is preached as an exhibition of talent; many a church is founded as a slap at some other church. Even missionary activity may become competitive, and soul winning may degenerate into a sort of brush-salesman project to satisfy the flesh. Do not forget, the Pharisees were great missionaries and would compass sea and land to make a convert.

A good way to avoid the snare of empty religious activity is to appear before God every once in a while with our Bibles open to the thirteenth chapter of First Corinthians. This passage, though rated one of the most beautiful in the Bible, is also one of the severest to be found in Sacred Writ. The apostle takes the highest religious service and consigns it to futility unless it is motivated by love. Lacking love, prophets, teachers, orators, philanthropists and martyrs are sent away without reward.

To sum it up, we may say simply that in the sight of God we are judged not so much by what we do as by our reasons for doing it. Not *what* but *why* will be the important question when we Christians appear at the judgment seat to give account of the deeds done in the body.

The Presence More Important Than the Program

It seems to me a significant, if not a positively ominous, thing that the words "program" and "programing" occur so frequently in the language of the church these days.

I am well aware that the words have been borrowed and adapted as expressing more nearly than any others the order of religious items on the agenda of the average church service. But the very fact that they lend themselves to the service so neatly is itself extremely disquieting to the few who still want to follow New Testament order in the public worship of God.

When we compare our present carefully programed meetings with the New Testament we are reminded of the remark of a famous literary critic after he had read Alexander Pope's translation of Homer's *Odyssey:* "It is a beautiful poem, but it is not Homer." So the fast-paced, highly spiced, entertaining service of today may be a beautiful example of masterful programing—but it is not a Christian service.

The two are leagues apart in almost every essential. About the only thing they have in common is the presence of a number of persons in one room. There the similarity ends and glaring dissimilarities begin.

For one thing, the object of attention is not the same in the two meetings.

Whether it be a communion service, morning worship, evangelistic meeting, prayer meeting or any other kind of true Christian gathering the center of attention will always be Christ. "Where two or three are gathered together in my name, there am I in the midst of them" (Mat. 18:20). These words of our Lord set the pattern for all Christian assemblies. Throughout the New Testament after Pentecost one marked characteristic of all Christian meetings was the believers' preoccupation with their risen Lord. Even the first Church Council (which might be called a "business" meeting if such a thing really existed in Bible times) was conducted in an atmosphere of great dignity and deep reverence. They talked of God and Christ and the Holy Ghost and the Scriptures and consecrated men who had hazarded their lives for the name of Jesus. They conferred for a while, then drew up a letter of instruction and sent it to the Gentile churches by the hand of Judas and Silas. It is of course unthinkable that such a meeting could have been held without some kind of agenda. Someone had to know what they had gathered to discuss.

The important point to be noticed, however, is that proceedings were carried on in an atmosphere of Christian worship. They lost sight of the program in the greater glory of a Presence.

Again, evangelistic and revival services in New Testament times were never divorced from worship. The Book of Acts is a record of evangelism and missionary activity, but the Presence is always there, and never for a moment do those early Christians forget it. Never do the disciples use gimmicks to attract crowds. They count on the power of the Spirit to see them through all the way. They gear their activities to Christ and are content to win or lose along with Him. The notion that they should set up a "programed" affair and use Jesus as a kind of sponsor never so much as entered their heads. To them Christ was everything. To them He was the object around which all revolved; He was, as He still is, Alpha and Omega, the beginning and the ending.

Christ was everything in the minds of those first believers, and that mighty fact dictated not only their conduct but their inner attitudes as well. Their mood, their demeanor, their expectations sprang out of their childlike conviction that Jesus was in the midst of them as Lord of creation, Head of the Church and High Priest of their profession.

Now, I freely admit that it is impossible to hold a Christian service without an agenda. If order is to be maintained, an order of service must exist somewhere. If two songs are to be sung, someone must know which one is to be sung first, and whether this knowledge is only in someone's head or has been reduced to paper there is indeed a "program," however we may dislike to call it that. The point we make here is that in our times the program has been substituted for the Presence. The program rather than the Lord of glory is the center of attraction. So the most popular gospel church in any city is likely to be the one that offers the most interesting program; that is, the church that can present the most and best features for the enjoyment of the public. These features are programed so as to keep everything moving and everybody expectant.

The evil of it all lies in its effect upon Christians and churches everywhere. Even persons who may honestly desire to serve God after the pattern shown us in the mount are deceived by the substitution of the program for the Presence, with the result that they never really become mature Christians. Their appetites are debauched and their sense of spiritual values dwarfed at the very beginning of their religious lives. Many of them go on year after year totally unaware that the program they go to see and hear each Sunday is not a Christian thing at all but a pagan concept superimposed upon the church by zealous but misled persons.

We'll do our churches a lot of good if we each one seek to cultivate the blessed Presence in our services. If we make Christ the supreme and constant object of devotion the program will take its place as a gentle aid to order in the public worship of God. If we fail to do this the program will finally obscure the Light entirely. And no church can afford that.

The World's Most Tragic Waste

One has only to travel over the surface of the earth a little to discover that God is extremely prodigal of material things. There appears to be a vast amount of almost everything: sand, prairies, mountains, lakes, seas, rocks, hills, plains, rivers, deserts, and only a tiny fraction of all these are of any use to mankind. The rest is, as far as we can see, wholly wasted.

There is on earth, however, one precious treasure which God is not willing to waste; that is human personality. Of this there is never a surplus. The sacred Scriptures are emphatic about God's regard for the human personality. It is written that God made man in His own image and likeness; not the soul or the spirit as a separate and superior part of man, but the whole living personality.

The tendency in popular thinking is to extract the soul from the total man and focus all attention upon it as the only thing about which God is concerned, and by inference the only thing about which we should concern ourselves. This has always appeared to me to be an extremely restricted view of things. Paul said, "Christ loved *me* and gave himself for *me*." The death of Christ was for the whole person, not for the soul only, and His invitation is to the entire man, the entire woman.

I think the whole modern notion embodied in our common phrase "soul winning" could stand a good overhauling in the light of the broader teachings of the Scriptures. True, the Proverb says "He that winneth souls is wise." But the word "souls" here stands for the whole man and not merely for his soul. The use of "soul" to mean a human being is common in the Bible. When Abraham set out for the land of Canaan he took with him Sarah, his wife, and Lot, his brother's son, and *the souls that they had gotten in Haran.* Is it not plain that these "souls" were persons whose names it did not suit the purpose of the narrative to give? Certainly they were people, not naked souls.

It is not my wish to create difficulties for the

pleasure of solving them, and it is altogether possible that thousands of zealous Christians use the expression "soul winning" while having in mind a true understanding of its broader meaning; but so powerful is human speech that the continued wrong use of a word or phrase may easily result in real error in thinking. If we would have a healthy grasp of truth we must see to it that we are semantically as well as theologically sound.

Human personality is dear to God because it is of all created things the nearest to being like Himself. Of nothing else is it said that it was created in "the likeness of God" (Gen. 5:1). Though alienated from God by sin and destined to perish, the fallen man is still nearer to God's likeness than any other creature upon earth. This makes it possible for him to receive regeneration and be fully restored to the fellowship of God, a privilege not enjoyed by those fallen beings of whom Peter and Jude and certain other Bible writers tell us. For this reason also the Word could become flesh and dwell among us. The Son could not take upon Him the nature of angels, but He could and did take on Him the seed of Abraham (Heb. 2:16).

These considerations tell us why God is willing to waste mountains but never willing to waste men; why He spends material things so prodigally and conserves human personality with such tender regard.

While God does not waste personality it is one
of the heavy tragedies of life that human personality
can waste itself. A man by his sin may waste himself, which is to waste that which on earth is most
like God. This is man's greatest tragedy, God's
heaviest grief.

Sin has many sides and many ramifications. It
is like a disease with numberless complications, any
one of which can kill the patient. It is lawlessness,
it is a missing of the mark, it is rebellion, it is per-
version, it is transgression; but it is also waste—a
frightful, tragic waste of the most precious of all
treasures. The man who dies out of Christ is said
to be lost, and hardly a word in the English tongue
expresses his condition with greater accuracy. He
has squandered a rare fortune and at the last he stands
for a fleeting moment and looks around, a moral fool,
a wastrel who has lost in one overwhelming and ir-
recoverable loss, his soul, his life, his peace, his total,
mysterious personality, his dear and everlasting all.

The Hunger of the Wilderness

"Man was made to dwell in a garden," says Dr. Harold C. Mason, "but through sin he has been forced to dwell in a field, a field which he has wrested from his enemies by sweat and tears, and which he preserves only at the price of constant watchfulness and endless toil. Let him but relax his efforts for a few years and the wilderness will claim his field again. The jungle and the forest will swallow his labors and all his loving care will have been in vain."

Every farmer knows the hunger of the wilderness, that hunger which no modern farm machinery, no improved agricultural methods, can ever quite destroy. No matter how well prepared the soil, how well kept the fences, how carefully painted the buildings, let the owner neglect for a while his prized and valued acres and they will revert again to the wild and be swallowed up by the jungle or the wasteland. The bias of nature is toward the wilderness, never toward the fruitful field. That, we repeat, every farmer knows.

To the alert Christian this fact will be more than

an observation of interest to farmers; it will be a parable, an object lesson setting forth a law that runs through all the regions of our fallen world, affecting things spiritual as well as things material. We cannot escape the law that would persuade all things to remain wild or to return to a wild state after a period of cultivation. What is true of the field is true also of the soul, if we are but wise enough to see it.

The moral bent of the fallen world is not toward godliness, but definitely away from it. "Is this vile world a friend to grace," asks the poet rhetorically, "to help me on to God?" The sad answer is *no,* and it would be well for us to see that each new Christian learn this lesson as soon as possible after his conversion. We sometimes leave the impression that it is possible to find at an altar of prayer, once and for all, purity of heart and power to assure victorious living for the rest of our days. How wrong this notion is has been proved by countless numbers of Christians through the centuries.

The truth is that no spiritual experience, however revolutionary, can exempt us from temptation; and what is temptation but the effort of the wilderness to encroach upon our new-cleared field? The purified heart is obnoxious to the devil and to all the forces of the lost world. They will not rest until they have won back what they have lost. The jungle will creep in and seek to swallow up the tiny areas that have been made free by the power of the Holy Ghost. Only watchfulness and constant prayer can preserve those moral gains won for us through the operations of God's grace.

The neglected heart will soon be a heart overrun with worldly thoughts; the neglected life will soon become a moral chaos; the church that is not jealously protected by mighty intercession and sacrificial labors will before long become the abode of every evil bird and the hiding place for unsuspected corruption. The creeping wilderness will soon take over that church that trusts in its own strength and forgets to watch and pray.

The law of the wilderness operates universally throughout our fallen world, on the mission field as well as in more sheltered lands. It is therefore an error to believe that our missionary obligation may be discharged by passing through one country after another and proclaiming the Gospel without following it up with thorough teaching and careful church organization. Yet this error is affecting large sections of the evangelical church, leading earnest persons to attempt to finish the evangelization of the world by this hit-and-skip method.

To make a few converts, only to leave them to their own devices without adequate care, is as foolish as to turn loose a flock of newborn lambs in the middle of a wilderness; it is as absurd as to clear and plant a field in the heart of the deep woods and to leave it to the mercies of undisciplined nature. All this would be a waste of effort and could not possibly result in any real gain.

So it is with any spiritual effort that does not take into account the hunger of the wilderness. The lambs must be shepherded or they will be killed; the field must be cultivated or it will be lost; spiritual gains must be conserved by watchfulness and prayer or they too will fall victim to the enemy.

Our Fruit Will Be What We Are

Water cannot rise above its own level. Neither can a Christian by any sudden spasmodic effort rise above the level of his own spiritual life.

I have seen under the sun how a man of God will let his tongue go all day in light and frivolous conversation, let his interest roam abroad among the idle pleasures of this world, and then, under the necessity of preaching at night, seek a last minute reprieve just before service and by cramming desperately in prayer try to put himself in a position where the spirit of the prophet will descend upon him as he enters the pulpit. By working himself up to an emotional white heat he may afterward have reason to congratulate himself that he had much liberty in preaching the Word. But he deceives himself and there is no wisdom in him. What he has been all day and all week is what he is when he opens his Bible to expound unto the people. Water cannot rise above its own level.

Men do not gather grapes of thorns, nor figs of thistles. The fruit of a tree is determined by the tree, and the fruit of life by the kind of life it is. What a man is interested in to the point of absorption both decides and reveals what kind of man he is; and the kind of man he is by a secret law of the soul decides the kind of fruit he will bear. The catch is that we are often unable to discover the true quality of our fruit until it is too late.

If we would be realistic in our Christian lives we must not overlook the tremendous power of affinity. By affinity I mean the sympathetic attraction which certain things and persons have for us. The human heart is extremely sensitive and altogether capable of setting up an inward relationship with objects far removed and forbidden. As the needle of the compass has an affinity for the north magnetic pole, so the heart can keep true to its secret love though separated from it by miles and years. What that loved object is may be discovered by observing which direction our thoughts turn when they are released from the hard restraints of work or study. Of what do we think when we are free to think of what we will? What object gives us inward pleasure as we brood over it? Over what do we muse in our free moments? To what does our imagination return again and again?

When we have answered these questions honestly we will know what kind of persons we are; and when we have discovered what kind of persons we are we may deduce the kind of fruit we will bear.

It is one of the clichés of the evangelist that the true worth of a church member is revealed by his life on Monday rather than on Sunday. There is a world of sober truth in the statement, and it is devoutly to be hoped that we who thus admonish others may ourselves remember to live the week through in the same atmosphere of sanctity that we desire so earnestly to inhabit on the Lord's Day.

It is written of Moses that he "went in before the Lord to speak with him . . . and he came out, and spake unto the children of Israel." This is the Biblical norm from which we depart to our own undoing and to the everlasting injury of the souls of men. No man has any moral right to go before the people who has not first been long before the Lord. No man has any right to speak to men about God who has not first spoken to God about men. And the prophet of God should spend more time in the secret place praying than he spends in the public place preaching.

As we dare not overlook the power of the human heart to establish affinities, so we dare not ignore the importance of the spiritual mood. Mood is mental weather. It is internal climate and it must be favorable to the growth of spiritual graces or they will not appear in the soul. The Christian who allows day after day a chilly climate to prevail in his heart need expect no grapes of Eshcol to hang over the wall when he goes before his Sunday school class, his choir, or his Sunday morning congregation.

One swallow does not make a spring nor one hot day a summer; nor will a few minutes of frantic praying before service bring out the tender buds or make the flowers to appear on the earth. The field must be soaked in sunshine over a long period before it will give forth its treasures. The Christian's heart must be soaked in prayer before the true spiritual fruits begin to grow. As the field has learned to live intimately and sympathetically with the rain and the sunshine, so must the Christian learn to live with God. We cannot in a brief time make up for the long neglect of God and things spiritual.

God's children live by laws as kind and as severe as those that govern nature. Grace operates within those laws but never contrary to them. , Our fruit will follow its native tree, and not all our frightened prayers can prevent it. If we would do holy deeds we must be holy men, every day and all the days that God grants us here below.

Needed: A Baptism of Clear Seeing

When reviewing the religious scene today we are tempted to fix on one or another weakness and say, "This is what is wrong with the Church. If this were corrected we could recapture the glory of the early Church and have Pentecostal times back with us again."

This tendency to oversimplification is itself a weakness and should be guarded against always, especially when dealing with anything as complex as religion as it occurs in modern times. It takes a very young man to reduce all our present woes to a single disease and cure the whole thing with one simple remedy. Older and wiser heads will be more cautious, having learned that the prescribed nostrum seldom works for the reason that the diagnosis has not been correct. Nothing is that simple. Few spiritual diseases occur alone. Almost all are complicated by the presence of others and are so vitally interrelated as they spread over the whole religious body that it would take the wisdom of a Solomon to find a single cure.

For this reason I am hesitant to point to any one defect in present day Christianity and make all our troubles to stem from it alone. That Bible religion in our times is suffering rapid decline is so evident as to need no proof; but just what has brought about this decline is not so easy to discover. I can only say that I have observed one significant lack among evangelical Christians which might turn out to be the real cause of most of our spiritual troubles; and of course if that were true, then the supplying of that lack would be our most critical need.

The great deficiency to which I refer is the lack of spiritual discernment, especially among our leaders. How there can be so much Bible knowledge and so little insight, so little moral penetration, is one of the enigmas of the religious world today. I think it is altogether accurate to say that there has never before been a time in the history of the Church when so many persons were engaged in Bible study as are so engaged today. If the knowledge of Bible doctrine were any guarantee of godliness, this would without doubt be known in history as the age of sanctity. Instead, it may well be known as the age of the Church's Babylonish captivity, or the age of worldliness, when the professed Bride of Christ allowed herself to be successfully courted by the fallen sons of men in unbelievable numbers. The body of evangelical believers, under evil influences, has during the last twenty-five years gone over to the world in complete and abject surrender, avoiding only a few of the grosser sins such as drunkenness and sexual promiscuity.

That this disgraceful betrayal has taken place in broad daylight with full consent of our Bible teachers and evangelists is one of the most terrible affairs in the spiritual history of the world. Yet I for one cannot believe that the great surrender was negotiated by men of evil heart who set out deliberately to destroy the faith of our Fathers. Many good and clean living persons have collaborated with the quislings who betrayed us. Why? The answer can only be: *from lack of spiritual vision.* Something like a mist has settled over the Church as "the face of the covering cast over all people, and the veil that is spread over all nations" (Isa. 25:7). Such a veil once descended upon Israel: "But their minds were blinded: for until this day remaineth the same veil untaken away in the reading of the old testament; which veil is done away in Christ. But even unto this day, when

109

Moses is read, the veil is upon their heart" (2 Cor. 3: 14, 15). That was Israel's tragic hour. God raised up the Church and temporarily disfranchised His ancient people. He could not trust His work to blind men.

Surely we need a baptism of clear seeing if we would escape the fate of Israel and of every other religious body in history that forsook God. If not the greatest need, then surely one of the greatest is for the appearance of Christian leaders with prophetic vision. We desperately need seers who can see through the mist. Unless they come soon it will be too late for this generation. And if they do come we will no doubt crucify a few of them in the name of our worldly orthodoxy. But the cross is always the harbinger of the resurrection.

Mere evangelism is not our present need. Evangelism does no more than extend religion, of whatever kind it may be. It gains acceptance for religion among larger numbers of people without giving much thought to the quality of that religion. The tragedy is that present day evangelism accepts the degenerate form of Christianity now current as the very religion of the apostles and busies itself with making converts to it with no questions asked. And all the time we are moving farther and farther from the New Testament pattern.

We must have a new reformation. There must

come a violent break with that irresponsible, amusement-mad, paganized pseudo religion which passes today for the faith of Christ and which is being spread all over the world by unspiritual men employing unscriptural methods to achieve their ends.

When the Roman Church apostatized, God brought about the Reformation. When the Reformation declined, God raised up the Moravians and the Wesleys. When these movements began to die God raised up Fundamentalism and the "deeper life" groups.

Now that these have almost without exception sold out to the world—what next?

Narrow Mansions

Any list of the spiritually great must include Augustine, Bishop of Hippo. A hundred informed men who might vote on who were the mightiest Christians since Paul would be likely to differ widely, but it is safe to assume that every one of them would mention Augustine. So great was he, intellectually and spiritually.

The ages have known how great a Christian Augustine was, but apparently he himself did not know. At the beginning of his famous devotional work, the *Confessions,* he says, "Narrow is the mansion of my soul; enlarge Thou it, that Thou mayest enter in." This was spoken in utter sincerity, and it may give us a hint of the secret of his greatness.

Augustine's vision of God was so tremendous that his own little capacity to receive seemed to him intolerably restricted. God was to him so vast, so world-filling, that no temple could contain Him, no shrine enclose Him. He fills heaven and the heaven of heavens, and the world itself is too small to receive Him. And when Augustine looked within his own heart he saw only narrowness and constriction; and it made him sick. "Enlarge Thou it!" was the involuntary cry of his soul.

How vastly different is this from the self-satisfied spirit we see everywhere these days. To be saved appears to be the highest ambition of most Christians today. To have eternal life and know it is the highest aspiration of many. Here they begin and here they end. Around this one theme they build their narrow temples, and in these cramped confines they sing their congratulatory songs and offer their cheery thanks.

The widest thing in the universe is not space; it is the potential capacity of the human heart. Being made in the image of God, it is capable of almost unlimited extension in all directions. And one of the world's worst tragedies is that we allow our hearts to shrink until there is room in them for little beside ourselves. Wordsworth lamented the fact that as we get older our world grows smaller and the "light that never was on land or sea" dims slowly down and goes out at last.

Heaven lies about us in our infancy!
Shades of the prison house begin to close
    Upon the growing boy,
But he beholds the light, and whence it flows.

   .   .   .   .

At length the man perceives it die away,
And fade into the light of common day.

Of all persons Christians should have the largest hearts; to them the narrowing of the heart should be an unthinkable calamity. They should seek for inner enlargement till their outward dimension gives no hint of the vastness within. To be great outwardly and small within is a kind of hypocrisy, but the modesty that hides a spacious interior under a simple exterior must be most pleasing to God.

One of the most stinging criticisms made against Christians is that their minds are narrow and their hearts small. This may not be wholly true, but that such a charge can be made at all is sufficient cause for serious heart searching and prayer. Godliness suggests Godlikeness, and to be Godlike is certainly to be magnanimous. God enfolds the world in His heart and contains the created universe. Restricted sympathies make us unlike God, and the bravest thing we can do is to admit it. Nothing is so futile as trying to defend our moral flaws against the sharp eyes of the world. We should remove the ground of the criticism rather than deny it.

Paul was a little man with a vast interior life; his great heart was often wounded by the narrowness of his disciples. The Christians at Corinth especially gave him much pain because of their inward constrictions. The sight of their shrunken souls hurt him too much, and he once burst out in a cry of mingled indignation and love, "Our mouth is open unto you, O Corinthians, our heart is enlarged. Ye are not straitened in us, but ye are straitened in your own affections. Now for a recompense in like kind (I speak as unto my children), be ye also enlarged" (2 Cor. 6:11-13, A.S.V.).

If any wonder how they can enlarge their hearts we hasten to tell them that they cannot do it. Paul said, "Be ye also enlarged," but he did not say, "Enlarge yourselves." That they could not do. Only God can work in the heart. The Architect and Builder of the soul alone can build it anew after the cyclone of sin has gone over it and left only one small room standing.

If we surrender our hearts to God we may expect a wondrous enlargement. And who knows what He can do if we take our hands off and let Him work? "How knowest thou what nobility God has bestowed on human nature," asks Meister Eckhart, "what perfections yet uncatalogued, aye, yet undiscovered?"

And one singular characteristic of the enlarging life is that it is quietly unaware of itself. The largest heart is likely to be heard praying, "Narrow is the mansion of my soul. Enlarge Thou it."

The Sanctification of Our Desires

In nature it is easy to watch the activity carried on by desire. The very perpetuation of the various species is guaranteed by the presence of desire, and each individual member of each species is sustained and nourished by the natural operation of desire. Every normal creature desires a mate, and so the perpetuation of life is achieved. Every creature desires food, and the life of each is supported. Thus desire is the servant of the God of nature and waits on His will.

115

In the moral world things are not otherwise. Right desires tend toward life and evil ones toward death. That in essence is the scriptural teaching on this subject. Whatever a man wants badly and persistently enough will determine the man's character. In the Pauline epistles the gravitational pull of the heart in one direction or another is called the "mind." In the eighth chapter of Romans, for instance, when Paul refers to the "mind" he is referring to the sum of our dominant desires. The mere intellect is not the mind: the mind is intellect plus an emotional tug strong enough to determine action.

By this definition it is easy to understand the words of Romans 8:5-7, "For they that are after the flesh do mind the things of the flesh; but they that are after the Spirit the things of the Spirit. For to be carnally minded is death; but to be spiritually minded is life and peace. Because the carnal mind is enmity against God: for it is not subject to the law of God, neither indeed can be." When our dominant desires are bad the whole life is bad as a consequence; when the desires are good the life comes up to the level of our desires, provided that we have within us the enabling Spirit.

At the root of all true spiritual growth is a set of right and sanctified desires. The whole Bible teaches that we can have whatever we want badly enough if, it hardly need be said, our desire is according to the will of God. The desire after God and holiness is back of all real spirituality, and when that desire becomes dominant in the life nothing can prevent us from having what we want. The longing cry of the God-hungry soul can be expressed in the five words of the song, "Oh, to be like Thee!" While this longing persists there will be steady growth in grace and a constant progress toward Christlikeness.

Unsanctified desire will stop the growth of any Christian life. Wrong desire perverts the moral judgment so that we are unable to appraise the desired object at its real value. However we try, still a thing looks morally better because we want it. For that reason our heart is often our worst counselor, for if it is filled with desire it may give us bad advice, pleading the purity of something that is in itself anything but pure.

As Christians our only safety lies in complete honesty. We must surrender our hearts to God so that we have no unholy desires, then let the Scriptures pronounce their judgment on a contemplated course. If the Scriptures condemn an object, we must accept that judgment and conform to it, no matter how we may for the moment feel about it.

To want a thing, or feel that we want it, and then to turn from it because we see that it is contrary to the will of God is to win a great battle on a field larger than Gettysburg or Bunker Hill. To bring our desires to the cross and allow them to be nailed there with Christ is a good and a beautiful thing. To be tempted and yet to glorify God in the midst of it is to honor Him where it counts. This is more pleasing to God than any amount of sheltered and untempted piety could ever be. To fight and to win in the name of Christ is always better than to have known no conflict.

God is always glorified when He wins a moral victory over us, and we are always benefited, immeasurably and gloriously benefited. The glory of God and the everlasting welfare of His people are always bound up together. The blood of Jesus Christ will cleanse not only actual sins which have been committed, but the very inward desires so that we will not want to sin. Purified desires will tend toward righteousness by a kind of gentle moral gravitation. Then it can be said that we are "spiritually minded." A blessed state indeed, and blessed are they that reach it.

In Praise of Disbelief

In our constant struggle to believe we are likely to overlook the simple fact that a bit of healthy disbelief is sometimes as needful as faith to the welfare of our souls.

I would go further and say that we would do well to cultivate a reverent skepticism. It will keep us out of a thousand bogs and quagmires where others who lack it sometimes find themselves. It is no sin to doubt some things, but it may be fatal to believe everything.

Faith is at the root of all true worship, and without faith it is impossible to please God. Through unbelief Israel failed to inherit the promises. "By grace are ye saved through faith." "The just shall live by faith." Such verses as these come trooping to our memories, and we wince just a little at the suggestion that unbelief may also be a good and useful thing. It sounds like a bold cancellation of the doctrine of faith as taught in the Scriptures and disposes us to write off the brazen advocate of disbelief as a Modernist. Let's look at the matter a bit more closely.

Faith never means gullibility. The man who believes everything is as far from God as the man who refuses to believe anything. Faith engages the Person and promises of God and rests upon them with perfect assurance. Whatever has behind it the character and word of the living God is accepted by faith as the last and final truth from which there must never be any appeal. Faith never asks questions when it has been established that God has spoken. "Yea, let God be true, but every man a liar" (Rom. 3:4). Thus faith honors God by counting Him righteous and accepts His testimony against the very evidence of its own senses. That is faith, and of such we can never have too much.

Credulity, on the other hand, never honors God, for it shows as great a readiness to believe anybody as to believe God Himself. The credulous person will accept anything as long as it is unusual, and the more unusual it is the more ardently he will believe. Any testimony will be swallowed with a straight face if it only has about it some element of the eerie, the preternatural, the unearthly. The gullible mentality is like the ostrich, that will gulp down anything that looks interesting—an orange, a tennis ball, a pocketknife opened or closed, a paper weight or a ripe apple. That he survives at all is a testimony not to his intelligence but to his tough constitution.

I have met Christians with no more discrimination than the ostrich. Because they must believe certain things, they feel that they must believe everything. Because they are called upon to accept the invisible they go right on to accept the incredible. God can and does work miracles; ergo, everything that passes for a miracle must be of God. God has spoken to men, therefore every man who claims to have had a revelation from God must be accepted as a prophet. Whatever is unearthly must be heavenly; whatever cannot be explained must be received as divine; the prophets were rejected, therefore everyone who is rejected is a prophet; the saints were misunderstood, so everyone who is misunderstood is a saint. This is the dangerous logic of the gullible Christian. And it can be as injurious as unbelief itself.

The healthy soul, like the healthy blood stream, has its proper proportion of white and red cells. The red corpuscles are like faith: they carry the life-giving oxygen to every part of the body. The white cells are like disbelief: they pounce upon dead and toxic matter and carry it out to the drain. Thus the two kinds of cells working together keep the tissues in good condition. In the healthy heart there must be provision for keeping dead and poisonous matter out of the life stream. This the credulous person never suspects. He is all for faith. He accents the affirmative and cultivates religious optimism to a point where he can no longer tell when he is being imposed upon.

Along with our faith in God must go a healthy disbelief of everything occult and esoteric. Numerology, astrology, spiritism, and everything weird and strange that passes for religion must be rejected. All this is toxic matter and has no place in the life of a true Christian. He will reject the whole business without compunction or fear. He has Christ, and He is the way, the truth and the life. What more does the Christian need?

Thankfulness As a Moral Therapeutic

In this world of corruption there is real danger that the earnest Christian may overreact in his resistance to evil and become a victim of the religious occupational disease, cynicism. The constant need to go counter to popular trends may easily develop in him a sour habit of faultfinding and turn him into a sulky critic of other men's matters, without charity and without love.

What makes this cynical spirit particularly dangerous is that the cynic is usually right. His analyses are accurate, his judgment sound. He can prove he is right in his moral views; yet for all that he is wrong, frightfully, pathetically wrong. But because he is right, he never suspects how tragically wrong he is. He slides imperceptibly into a condition of chronic bitterness and comes at last to accept it as normal.

It would be convenient indeed if it were possible to have a spiritual experience at some altar of prayer that would cure this condition completely and for good. And some sincere persons seem to believe that it is. I do not think so. It is like trying to get an infusion of health once for all that would take care of our physical condition for the rest of our lives, obviously an impossible thing. No matter how healthy we are, unless we cultivate correct bodily habits we will not stay healthy long. And an experience of heart cleansing that is not followed by right spiritual habits will be disappointing in the end. Continued spiritual health will result from right heart habits. If these are neglected the inner life will degenerate, no matter how wonderful our past experiences may have been.

Now, as a cure for the sour, faultfinding attitude I recommend the cultivation of the habit of thankfulness. Thanksgiving has great curative power. The heart that is constantly overflowing with gratitude will be safe from those attacks of resentfulness and gloom that bother so many religious persons. A thankful heart cannot be cynical.

I do not here recommend any of the applied-psychology nostrums so popular in liberal circles and among starry-eyed poets of the sweetness-and-light school of religious thought. The output of the "hear no evil, see no evil, speak no evil" jockeys makes painful reading for the man or woman who has been introduced to God through the miracle of the new birth. But I do recommend the cultivation of gratitude as a cure for spiritual sourness. There is good scriptural authority for this and experience teaches us that it works.

We should never take any blessing for granted, but accept everything as a gift from the Father of Lights. Whole days may be spent occasionally in the holy practice of being thankful. We should write on a tablet one by one the things for which we are grateful to God and to our fellow men. And a constant return to this thought during the day as our minds get free will serve to fix the habit in our hearts.

We could begin with our creation and tell God how grateful we are that He ever thought of us and brought us into being out of the empty void of nothingness. And when we had sinned, He remembered us still and sent His Son to die for us. He gave us the Bible and His blessed Spirit to teach us inwardly to understand it. We could go on to tell Him how glad we are for the Church, for good spiritual teachers, for faithful pastors and hymnists who have made the services of the Church each Sunday such a helpful and precious thing.

In trying to count our many blessings the difficulty is not to find things to count, but to find time to enumerate them all. Personally I have gotten great help from the practice of talking over with God the many kindnesses I have received from my fellow men. To my parents I owe my life and my upbringing. To my teachers I owe that patient line-upon-line instruction that took me when I was a young, ignorant pagan and enabled me to read and write. To the patriots and statesmen of the past I owe the liberties I now enjoy. To numerous and unknown soldiers who shed their blood to keep our country free I owe a debt I can never pay. And I please God and enlarge my own heart when I remind the Lord that I am grateful for them. For every man and woman of every race and nationality who may have contributed anything to my peace and welfare I am grateful, and I shall not let God forget that I am.

Understanding Those Dry Spells

Probably nothing else bothers the earnest Christian quite so much as the problem of those dry spells that come to him occasionally, no matter how faithfully he tries to obey God and walk in the light. He can never predict them and he cannot explain them. And there lies his difficulty.

It might comfort one who finds himself in the middle of an emotional desert to know that his experience is not unique. The sweetest and holiest saints whose feet have graced this earth have at some time found themselves there. The books of devotion which have come to us from the past almost all have at least one chapter dealing with what some of them call "aridity" in the Christian life. The very word itself tempts us to smile in sympathy, for it so perfectly describes the experience so many of us know only too well. Our heart feels "arid" and nothing we can do will bring the rain. It is good to know during such an internal drought that it has been a common experience with the saints.

One reason for our distress at such times is the

knowledge that sin is one cause of aridity in the life; we naturally reason that if sin brings drought and we are suffering a dry spell, then we must have been guilty of sin whether we know it or not. The way to deal with the problem is to remember that *sin is not the only cause of dryness.* If after an honest examination of our lives we are sure that we are not living in a state of disobedience and that no past sin is unforgiven, we may dismiss sin as the cause of our dry condition. We do God no honor and ourselves no good by assuming that we have sinned if we have not. Indeed we play straight into Satan's hands by accepting the morbid suggestion that somewhere in the mysterious depths of our nature there must be some sin that is displeasing God and causing Him to hide His face from us. What God has cleansed we should not call unclean; to do so would be unbelief.

"Religion," say the theologians, "lies in the will." What our will is set to do is what really matters at last. Aridity has nothing to do with the will. "If any man will," said Jesus; He did not say "If any man feel." Feeling is the play of emotion over the will, a kind of musical accompaniment to the business of living, and while it is indeed most enjoyable to have the band play as we march to Zion it is by no means indispensable. We can work and walk without music and if we have true faith we can walk with God without feeling.

127

Normally we may expect some degree of spiritual joy to be present most of the time. Fellowship with God is so delightful that it cannot but provide a large measure of joy; but we are talking now about those times when our joy fades out and the presence of the Lord is felt only feebly or not at all. Such times demand that we exercise faith. Moments of great spiritual delight do not require much faith; if we never came down from the mount of blessing we might easily come to trust in our own delights rather than in the unshakeable character of God. It is necessary therefore that our watchful Heavenly Father withdraw His inward comforts from us sometimes to teach us that Christ alone is the Rock upon which we must repose our everlasting trust.

About Hindrances

The notion that hostile persons or unfavorable circumstances can prevent the will of God from being fulfilled in a human life is altogether erroneous. Nothing, no one, can hinder God or a good man.

It is one of the glories of the Christian faith that it can be present in effective power regardless of whether or not the moral and political environment is favorable to it. H. G. Wells said somewhere that he personally believed Buddhism to be the best religion, but admitted that it could flourish only in countries having a warm climate! I once heard a Catholic priest lament the plight of another priest who had been thrown into jail in Nazi Germany "and forbidden to practice his religion." It sounded oddly humorous at the time; yet I can understand how a religion that lay mostly in external observances could be forbidden. If true religion consisted in outward practices, then it could be destroyed by laws forbidding those practices. But if the true worshiper is one who worships God in spirit and in truth, how can laws or jails or abuses or deprivations prevent the spiritual man from worshiping?

Let a man set his heart only on doing the will of God and he is instantly free. No one can hinder him. If we understand our first and sole duty to consist of loving God supremely and loving everyone, even our enemies, for God's dear sake, then we can enjoy spiritual tranquillity under every circumstance; or if tribulations harrow our souls, still we can rest in the deep assurance that we are doing the will of God and that He is accepting our very sufferings as a sweet sacrifice, well pleasing in His sight.

It is only when we introduce our own will into our relation to God that we get into trouble. When we weave into the pattern of our lives threads of our own selfish desires we instantly become subject to hindrances from the outside. If I mingle some pet religious enterprise of mine with the will of God and come to think of them as one, I can be hindered in my religious life. Then I'll begin to blame whoever stands in my way and excuse my spiritual breakdowns as being caused by someone or something that is working to "hinder" me.

The essence of spiritual worship is to love supremely, to trust confidently, to pray without ceasing and to seek to be Christlike and holy and to do all the good we can for Christ's sake. How impossible for anyone to hinder that kind of "practice." As soon as our normal churchgoing religion is interdicted by government decree or made for the time impossible by circumstances we can retire to the sanctuary of our own hearts and worship God acceptably till He sees fit to change the circumstances and allow us to resume the outward practice of our faith. But the fire has not gone out on the altar of our heart in the meantime and we have learned the sweet secret of submission and trust, a lesson we could not have learned any other way.

If we find ourselves irked by external hindrances, be sure we are victims of our own self-will. Nothing can hinder the heart that is fully surrendered and quietly trusting, because nothing can hinder God.

The Uses of Suffering

The Bible has a great deal to say about suffering and most of it is encouraging.

The prevailing religious mood is not favorable to the doctrine, but anything that gets as much space as the doctrine of suffering gets in the Scriptures should certainly receive careful and reverent attention from the sons of the new creation. We cannot afford to neglect it, for whether we understand it or not we are going to experience some suffering. As human beings we cannot escape it.

From the first cold shock that brings a howl of protest from the newborn infant down to the last anguished gasp of the aged man, pain and suffering dog our footsteps as we journey here below. It will pay us to learn what God says about it so that we may know how to act and what to expect when it comes.

Christianity embraces everything that touches the

life of man, and deals with it all effectively. Because
suffering is a real part of human life, Christ Himself
took part in the same and learned obedience by the
things which He suffered. It is not possible that
the afflicted saint should feel a stab of pain to which
Christ is a stranger. Our Lord not only suffered once
on earth, He suffers now along with His people. "Behold," cried the old saint as he watched a youthful
martyr die, "Behold how our Lord suffers in the body
of His handmaid."

> *Think not thou canst sigh a sigh*
> *And thy Maker is not by;*
> *Think not thou canst weep a tear*
> *And thy Maker is not near.*

There is a kind of suffering which profits no one:
it is the bitter and defiant suffering of the lost. The
man out of Christ may endure any degree of affliction
without being any the wiser or the better for it. It
is for him all a part of the tragic heritage of sin, a
kind of earnest of the pains of hell. To such there
is not much that we can say and for such there is
little that we can do except to try in the name of
Christ and our common humanity to reduce the suffering as much as we can. That much we owe to all
the children of misfortune, whatever their color or race
or creed.

As long as we remain in the body we shall be

subject to a certain amount of that common suffering which we must share with all the sons of men—loss, bereavement, nameless heartaches, disappointments, partings, betrayals and griefs of a thousand sorts. This is the less profitable kind of suffering, but even this can be made to serve the followers of Christ. There is such a thing as consecrated griefs, sorrows that may be common to everyone but which take on a special character for the Christian when accepted intelligently and offered to God in loving submission. We should be watchful lest we lose any blessing which such suffering might bring.

But there is another kind of suffering, known only to the Christian: it is voluntary suffering deliberately and knowingly incurred for the sake of Christ. Such is a luxury, a treasure of fabulous value, a source of riches beyond the power of the mind to conceive. And it is rare as well as precious, for there are few in this decadent age who will of their own choice go down into this dark mine looking for jewels. But of our own choice it must be, for there is no other way to get down. God will not force us into this kind of suffering; He will not lay this cross upon us nor embarrass us with riches we do not want. Such riches are reserved for those who apply to serve in the legion of the expendables, who love not their lives unto the death, who volunteer to suffer for Christ's sake and who follow up their application with lives that challenge the devil and invite the fury of hell. Such as these have said good-bye to the world's toys; they have chosen to suffer affliction with the people of God; they have accepted toil and suffering as their earthly portion. The marks of the cross are upon them and they are known in heaven and in hell.

But where are they? Has this breed of Christian died out of the earth? Have the saints of God joined the mad scramble for security? Has the cross become no more than a symbol, a bloodless and sterile relic of nobler times? Are we now afraid to suffer and unwilling to die? I hope not, but I wonder. And only God has the answer.

Praise God for the Furnace

It was the enraptured Rutherford who could shout in the midst of serious and painful trials, "Praise God for the hammer, the file and the furnace."

The hammer is a useful tool, but the nail, if it had feeling and intelligence, could present another side of the story. For the nail knows the hammer only as an opponent, a brutal, merciless enemy who lives to pound it into submission, to beat it down out of sight and clinch it into place. That is the nail's view of the hammer, and it is accurate except for one thing: The nail forgets that both it and the hammer are servants of the same workman. Let the nail but remember that the hammer is held by the workman and all resentment toward it will disappear. The carpenter decides whose head shall be beaten next and what hammer shall be used in the beating. That is his sovereign right. When the nail has surrendered to the will of the workman and has gotten a little glimpse of his benign plans for its future it will yield to the hammer without complaint.

The file is more painful still, for its business is to bite into the soft metal, scraping and eating away the edges till it has shaped the metal to its will. Yet the file has, in truth, no real will in the matter, but serves another master as the metal also does. It is the master and not the file that decides how much shall be eaten away, what shape the metal shall take, and how long the painful filing shall continue. Let the metal accept the will of the master and it will not try to dictate when or how it shall be filed.

As for the furnace, it is the worst of all. Ruthless and savage, it leaps at every combustible thing that enters it and never relaxes its fury till it has reduced it all to shapeless ashes. All that refuses to burn is melted to a mass of helpless matter, without will or purpose of its own. When everything is melted that will melt and all is burned that will burn, then and not till then the furnace calms down and rests from its destructive fury.

With all this known to him, how could Rutherford find it in his heart to praise God for the hammer, the file and the furnace? The answer is simply that he loved the Master of the hammer, he adored the Workman who wielded the file, he worshiped the Lord who heated the furnace for the everlasting blessing of His children. He had felt the hammer till its rough beatings no longer hurt; he had endured the file till he had come actually to enjoy its bitings; he had walked with God in the furnace so long that it had become as his natural habitat. That does not overstate the facts. His letters reveal as much.

Such doctrine as this does not find much sympathy among Christians in these soft and carnal days. We tend to think of Christianity as a painless system by which we can escape the penalty of past sins and attain to heaven at last. The flaming desire to be rid of every unholy thing and to put on the likeness of Christ at any cost is not often found among us. We expect to enter the everlasting kingdom of our Father and to sit down around the table with sages, saints and martyrs; and through the grace of God, maybe we shall; yes, maybe we shall. But for the most of us it could prove at first an embarrassing experience. Ours might be the silence of the untried soldier in the presence of the battle-hardened heroes who have fought the fight and won the victory and who have scars to prove that they were present when the battle was joined.

The devil, things and people being what they are, it is necessary for God to use the hammer, the file and the furnace in His holy work of preparing a saint for true sainthood. It is doubtful whether God can bless a man greatly until He has hurt him deeply.

Without doubt we of this generation have become too soft to scale great spiritual heights. Salvation has come to mean deliverance from unpleasant things. Our hymns and sermons create for us a religion of consolation and pleasantness. We overlook the place of the thorns, the cross and the blood. We ignore the function of the hammer and the file.

Strange as it may sound, it is yet true that much of the suffering we are called upon to endure on the highway of holiness is an inward suffering for which scarcely an external cause can be found. For our journey is an inward journey, and our real foes are invisible to the eyes of men. Attacks of darkness, of despondency, of acute self-depreciation may be endured without any change in our outward circumstances. Only the enemy and God and the hardpressed Christian know what has taken place. The inward suffering has been great and a mighty work of purification has been accomplished, but the heart knoweth its own sorrow and no one else can share it. God has cleansed His child in the only way He can, circumstances being what they are. Thank God for the furnace.

Victory in the Guise of Defeat

"Our Lord Himself, St. Peter and St. Paul appeared to have been defeated."
—DE TOURVILLE.

It is often difficult to tell in a given instance whether we have been defeated or are victorious in a conflict. Sometimes what looks like a defeat will be seen later to have been a positive victory.

When Joseph was sold into slavery, the end appeared to have come for the young dreamer. Years later when the deep ways of God had come to light he could say to his now repentant brethren, "Ye thought evil against me; but God meant it unto good, to bring to pass, as it is this day, to save much people alive." Joseph's humiliating defeat had turned into personal victory for him and preservation for his entire family. God *might* have accomplished the same end in a different way. All we know is that He did not.

When the three Hebrew children disappeared into the seven-times-heated furnace no doubt many who watched turned away shaking their heads in pity; but things looked different the next moment when the king discovered that the men of God were preserved whole without the smell of fire upon them. Shadrach, Meshach and Abed-nego had not been sure how the whole thing would turn out. They had told the king boldly, "God whom we serve is able to deliver us from the burning fiery furnace, and he will deliver us out of thine hand, O king. But if not, be it known unto thee, O king, that we will not serve thy gods." And possibly for one breathless minute they thought their time had come. But God saw otherwise and turned their defeat into victory.

And it must not be forgotten that this principle works just the same in reverse. When David had succeeded in stealing Uriah's wife he no doubt felt he had scored a real conquest, but subsequent events showed instead that he had suffered a stunning defeat. He was never the same after his "conquest." What the armies of the alien could never do on the field, David himself accomplished by one act of wrong-

139

doing; that is, he brought about his own defeat. When he met Goliath he turned what looked like defeat into victory. When he met Bathsheba he turned a long record of victories into shameful defeat.

One thing about all this is that we cannot always be sure at the time just who is winning unless we keep our hearts very pure and our minds cool and God-possessed. When the soldiers of Pilate flung Christ to the ground and began to drive in the nails, everything looked as if our Lord had ended a failure. Surely this ignominious death would not come to a man of God. There must be some mistake. The man Jesus had been an idealist, a visionary, but now His hopes and the hopes of His followers were collapsing under the brutal attacks of tough, practical men. So reasoned the onlookers. But our Lord could die with the same calm in which He had lived. He had known all along how things would turn out. He had looked beyond the cross to the triumphant resurrection. He knew His apparent defeat would eventuate in universal glory for the human race.

Love of the Unseen Is Possible

"Jesus Christ: whom having not seen, ye love" (1 Pet. 1:7, 8).

If Peter had said "Whom having not *known* ye love" he would have spoken an impossibility, but the inspired pen of the apostle wrote accurately. There are laws of the mind which can never be violated; it is a tribute to the perfection of the Scriptures that they never create a situation contrary to those laws. It is not psychologically possible to love anyone we have not known in some measure of experience. "Lord, Thou alone seest and knowest the nature of a loving heart," wrote Henry Suso, "and Thou knowest that no one can love what he can in no wise understand."

That it is altogether possible to love persons we have not seen is proved in everyday experience. A blind mother, for instance, will cuddle her baby to her heart with all the shining-eyed delight of a normal, seeing woman. Yet she has not seen her baby. How can this be? The answer is that though she has not seen him she has *experienced* him in a dozen sweet and intimate ways. She has felt his soft, smooth skin, heard his whimpers and gurgles, smelled the gentle baby fragrances so dear to the heart of all mothers, felt the warmth of his little body against hers. She has *known* him, and because she has known him she can say, "Whom having not seen I love."

But it is wholly impossible to love the unknown. There must be some degree of experience before there can be any degree of love. Perhaps this accounts for the coldness toward God and Christ evidenced by the average Christian. How can we love a Being whom we have not heard nor felt nor experienced? We may work up some kind of reverence for the noble ideals the thought of God brings to our minds; we may feel a certain awe when we think of the high and holy One that inhabiteth eternity; but what we feel is hardly love. It is rather an appreciation of the sublime, a response of the heart to the mysterious and the grand. It is good and desirable, but it is not love.

The command to love God with our whole being has seemed to many persons to be impossible of fulfillment. And it may be properly argued that we cannot love by fiat. Love is too gentle, too frail a creature to spring up at the command of another. It would be like commanding the barren tree to bring forth fruit or the winter forest to be green. What then can it mean?

The answer is found in the nature of man and

142

of God. God being who He is must have obedience from His creatures. Man being who he is must render that obedience. And he owes God complete obedience whether or not he feels for Him the faintest trace of love in his heart. It is a question of the sovereign right of God to require His creatures to obey Him. Man's first and basic sin was disobedience. When he disobeyed God he violated the claims of divine love with the result that love for God died within him. Now, what can he do to restore that love to his heart again? The answer to that question is given in one word: *Repent.*

The heart that mourns its coldness toward God needs only to repent its sins, and a new, warm and satisfying love will flood into it. For the act of repentance will bring a corresponding act of God in self-revelation and intimate communion. Once the seeking heart finds God in personal experience there will be no further problem about loving Him. To know Him is to love Him and to know Him better is to love Him more.

Those who have dealt with the ugly problem of sin in their own hearts will find no difficulty with the doctrine of God and His present invisibility. They do not see Him, it is true, but they experience Him in a thousand inward encounters. They can say with true conviction, "Jesus Christ is He whom having not seen I love."

143

Something Beyond Song

There is a notion widely held among Christians that song is the highest possible expression of the joy of the Lord in the soul of a man.

That idea is so near to being true that it may seem spiritually rude to challenge it. I have no wish to pick theological lint nor to pluck the wings off religious flies for the thrill such a sadistic act might afford. There are probably hundreds of wrong notions in all of our heads, notions that, while they are wrong, are still too insignificant to deserve attention. They are like the minor physical blemishes which we all have, harmless if not beautiful, and altogether too trivial to rate mention by serious-minded persons.

The idea, however, that song is the supreme expression of all and any possible spiritual experience is not small; it is large and meaningful and needs to be brought to the test of the Scriptures and Christian testimony.

Both the Bible and the testimony of a thousand saints show that there is experience beyond song.

There are delights which the heart may enjoy in the awesome presence of God which cannot find expression in language; they belong to the unutterable element in Christian experience. Not many enjoy them because not many know that they can. The whole concept of ineffable worship has been lost to this generation of Christians. Our level of life is so low that no one expects to know the deep things of the soul until the Lord returns. So we are content to wait, and while we wait we are wont to cheer our hearts sometimes by breaking into song.

Far be it from us to discourage the art of singing. Creation itself took its rise in a burst of song; Christ rose from the dead and sang among His brethren, and we are promised that they who dwell in dust will rise and sing at the resurrection. The Bible is a musical book and, next to the Scriptures themselves, the best book to own is a good hymnbook. But still there is something beyond song.

The Bible and Christian biography make a great deal of silence, but we of today make of it exactly nothing. The average service in gospel circles these days is kept alive by noise. By making a lot of religious din we assure our faltering hearts that everything is well and, conversely, we suspect silence and regard it as a proof that the meeting is "dead." Even the most devout seem to think they must storm heaven with loud outcries and mighty bellowings or their

145

prayers are of no avail. Not all silence is spiritual. Some Christians are silent because they have nothing to say; others because what they have to say cannot be uttered by mortal tongue. Of the first we do not speak at the moment, but confine our remarks to the latter.

Where the Holy Spirit is permitted to exercise His full sway in a redeemed heart the progression is likely to be as follows: First, voluble praise, in prose speech or prayer or witness; then, when the crescendo rises beyond the ability of studied speech to express, comes song; when song breaks down under the weight of glory, then comes silence where the soul, held in deep fascination, feels itself blessed with an unutterable beatitude.

At the risk of being written off as an extremist or a borderline fanatic we offer it as our mature opinion that more spiritual progress can be made in one short moment of speechless silence in the awesome presence of God than in years of mere study. While our mental powers are in command there is always the veil of nature between us and the face of God. It is only when our vaunted wisdom has been met and defeated in a breathless encounter with Omniscience that we are permitted really to know, when prostrate and wordless the soul receives divine knowledge like a flash of light on a sensitized plate. The exposure may be brief, but the results are permanent.

146

Three Degrees of Love

The phrase "the love of God," when used by Christians, almost always refers to God's love for us. We must remember that it can also mean our love for God.

The first and greatest commandment is that we should love God with all the power of our total personality. Though all love originates in God and is for that reason God's own love, yet we are permitted to catch and reflect back that love in such manner that it becomes our love indeed, in much the same way that sunlight reflected from the moon becomes moonlight.

The Christian's love for God has by some religious thinkers been divided into two kinds, the love of gratitude and the love of excellence.

The love that springs out of gratitude is found in such passages as Psalm 116:1, "I love the Lord, because he hath heard my voice and my supplications," and First John 4:19, "We love him, because he first loved us." This is an entirely proper and legitimate kind of love and is quite acceptable to God even though it is among the most elementary and immature of the religious emotions. Love that is the result of gratitude for favors received cannot but have a certain element of selfishness in it. At least it is on the borderline of selfishness and is difficult to distinguish from it, the blunt fact being that it is roused only by benefits received and does not exist apart from them.

A higher kind of love is the love of excellence. This love is awakened by consideration of God's glorious Being, and has in it a strong element of admiration. "My beloved is white and ruddy, the chiefest among ten thousand. His mouth is most sweet: yea, he is altogether lovely" (Song of Solomon 5:10, 16).

This love of the divine excellencies differs from the love that springs from gratitude in that its reasons are more elevated and the element of selfishness is reduced almost to the vanishing point. We should note, however, that the two have one thing in common: they can both give a reason for their existence. Love that can offer reasons is a rational thing and has not attained to a state of complete purity. It is not perfect love.

We must carry our love to God further than love of gratitude and love of excellence. There is an advanced stage of love which goes far beyond either.

Down on the level of the merely human it is altogether common to find love that rises above both gratitude and admiration. The mother of a subnormal child, for instance, may love her unfortunate child with an emotional attachment altogether impossible to understand. The child excites no gratitude in her breast, for all the benefits have flowed the other way; the helpless infant has been nothing but a burden from the time it was born. Neither can the mother find in such a child any excellence to admire, for there is none. Yet her love is something wonderful and terrible to see. Her tender feelings have swallowed the child and assimilated it to her own inward being to such a degree that she feels herself one with it. And indeed she is one with it emotionally. Her life and that of the child are more certainly united than they were during that sacred period before she gave it birth. For always the union achieved by hearts is more beautiful than anything that can be experienced by flesh and blood.

The sum of what we say here is that there is in the higher type of love a suprarational element that cannot and does not attempt to give reasons for its existence. It says not "I love because"; it only whispers "I love." Perfect love knows no *because.*

There is a place in the religious experience where we love God for Himself alone, with never a thought of His benefits. And there is a place where the heart does not reason from admiration to affection. True, it all may begin lower down, but it quickly rises to the height of blind adoration where reason is suspended and the heart worships in unreasoning blessedness. It can only exclaim, "Holy, holy, holy," while scarcely knowing what it means.

If this should all seem too mystical, too unreal, we offer no proof and make no effort to defend our position. This can be understood only by those who have experienced it. By the rank and file of present day Christians it will be rejected or shrugged off as preposterous. So be it. Some will read and will recognize an accurate description of the sunlit peaks where they have been for at least brief periods and to which they long often to return. And such will need no proof.

We Need Cool Heads

In the Church of God two opposite dangers are to be recognized and avoided; they are a cold heart and a hot head. And for downright harmful effects the hot head is often the worse of the two.

The human heart is heretical by nature, and unless well instructed by the Scriptures and fully enlightened by the indwelling Spirit it is sure to introduce some of its own notions into its religious beliefs and practices. It may, for instance, confuse the fervor of the Spirit with the heat of the flesh, and mistake the scintillations of the overheated imagination for the glow of the true Shekinah. And this can be extremely dangerous, especially when it is found among religious leaders.

It is true that Ezekiel on one occasion went in the heat of his spirit; but there is no hint that his mind was anything but calm, for he said also that "the hand of the Lord was strong upon me." The steadying hand of God prevents the fever of the human spirit from affecting the critical faculties and leading to extreme and unwise conduct.

In our commendable eagerness to see the fires of Pentecost burn again among us we are guilty sometimes of overstating the facts. For instance, we habitually point to the fervor of the great saints, their passionate love, their flaming desire, and fail entirely to notice another characteristic of their personalities, viz., their calm steady judgment and salty good sense. For it cannot be denied that the reformers, the revivalists, the mystics of yesterday, were for the most part uncommonly poised and self-possessed men. The heat of John Wesley's spirit can still be felt after the passing of the years, but whoever will take the trouble to read his writings will find that he was capable of exercising

151

the calmest and most balanced judgment concerning just about everything. The same may be said of Finney and a host of others whose examples are used today to stimulate the cold hearts of our time to seek after heavenly fire.

It may be said without qualification that there can never be too much fire, if it is the true fire of God; and it can be said as certainly that there cannot be too much cool judgment in religious matters if that judgment is sanctified by the Spirit. The history of revivals in the Church reveals how harmful the hot head can be. Hardly a revival visited the Church but was stopped in its tracks by the very persons who were trying to promote it. When a spiritual movement becomes large enough to get out from under the direction of the ones God used to originate it, then the danger begins. Extremists who rode to local fame on the wave of revival power now take over; immediately everything goes out of focus. What before was incidental now becomes fundamental; what was a by-product now becomes the main product. What had been present as something temporary and undesirable is now promoted as being itself the very mark of God on the movement. How many revivals have been killed in this way the records will abundantly show. And many of us know of such instances within our own narrow field of experience which have never gotten into the record at all.

Among the gifts of the Spirit scarcely any one is of greater practical usefulness than the gift of discernment. This gift should be highly valued and frankly sought as being almost indispensable in these critical times. This gift will enable us to distinguish the chaff from the wheat and to divide the manifestations of the flesh from the operations of the Spirit. For want of this gift many of God's good people continue to chase fireflies in the mistaken belief that they are following the fire and cloud. And this they do to the great harm of their own souls and to the confusion of others.

There will always be those who hesitate to believe that anything is of God unless it has about it some flavor of the weird, or at least of the supernatural. Persons with a certain type of mentality think only in extremes; they can never achieve perspective in anything, but see everything so close as to miss entirely the corrective benefits of distance. They will believe anything as long as it is unusual and just a little mysterious. Their fire is not large, but by holding it always on one fine point they manage to generate a surprising amount of heat, only at that one point.

The priests of the sanctuary, when they went in to sacrifice, were not permitted to wear "any thing that causeth sweat." Human sweat can add nothing to the work of the Spirit, especially when it is nerve sweat. The hottest fire of God is cool when it touches the redeemed intellect. It makes the heart glow but leaves the judgment completely calm.

These are days of great religious turmoil. We do well to remember that "God hath not given us the spirit of fear; but of power, and of love, and of a sound mind." Let love burn on with increasing fervor but bring every act to the test of quiet wisdom. Keep the fire in the furnace where it belongs. An overheated chimney will create more excitement than a well controlled furnace, but it is likely to burn the house down. Let the rule be: a hot furnace but a cool chimney.

We Can Afford to Wait

The world do move, they say, and times change. And this bromide, or another like it and just as bad, is supposed to justify the habit of denouncing everything old and taking up everything new, no one apparently stopping to consider that often the only fault to be found with the one is that it is old and the only virtue attaching to the other is that it is new.

One thing seems to be quite forgotten: the world moves and times change but people remain the same always. Just as a pendulum remains fixed at the top while it swings back and forth from one extreme to another, so the human race remains basically unchanged while it moves through its limited arc. Men are always the same while they change, like styles in ladies' clothes; whatever the fashion is today, wait a bit and it will be back where it was a few years ago. And the "new" style will be hailed as enthusiastically as if it had not been all the rage only a short while before.

No responsible person will deny that some changes made by the race over the years have been improvements, and so may have represented progress and advance, though just what we are supposed to be advancing toward has not been made very clear by our leaders. And it would seem to be difficult to show that we are moving toward an end when we do not know what or where that end is, or even if such an end exists at all.

To a Christian, conditioned as he is to observing life from above and judging all things in the light of eternal values, the modern feverish devotion to the newest invention and the latest happening seems more than a little ridiculous. The only parallel we can think of at the moment is that of a deadly serious and fanatically-determined dachshund chasing breathlessly after its tail, a tail, incidentally, which is not there because it has previously been removed. Add a large number of other dachshunds, bespectacled and solemn, writing books to prove that the frustrated puppy's activity is progress, and you have the picture.

Christians have often been accused of being reactionary because they cannot get up any enthusiasm over the latest scheme that someone thinks up to bring in the millennium. They will not mount up and go galloping off in all directions every time some come-lately patron of circular progress delivers a speech; and the world cannot forgive them.

Well, it is not to be wondered at. A real Christian is an odd number anyway. He feels supreme love for One whom he has never seen, talks familiarly every day to Someone he cannot see, expects to go to heaven on the virtue of Another, empties himself in order to be full, admits he is wrong so he can be declared right, goes down in order to get up, is strongest when he is weakest, richest when he is poorest, and happiest when he feels worst. He dies so he can live, forsakes in order to have, gives away so he can keep, sees the invisible, hears the inaudible, and knows that which passeth knowledge. And all the while he may be confounding his critics by his unbelievable practicality: his farm may be the most productive, his business the best managed, and his mechanical skill the sharpest of anyone in his neighborhood.

The man who has met God is not looking for something—he has found it; he is not searching for light—upon him the Light has already shined. His certainty may seem bigoted, but his is the assurance of one who knows by experience. His religion is not hearsay; he is not a copy, not a facsimile print; he is an original from the hand of the Holy Ghost.

We have not here described a superior saint— merely a true Christian, far from perfect and with much yet to learn; but his firsthand acquaintance with God saves him from the nervous scramble in which the world is engaged and which is popularly touted as progress.

No doubt we shall yet hear many a tin whistle and see many a parade bravely marching off toward the Four Freedoms or the Universal Brotherhood of Mankind or the Age of Atomic Progress, and we will be expected to fall into step. Let's be cautious. We are waiting for a trumpet note that will call us away from the hurly-burly and set in motion a series of events that will result at last in a new heaven and a new earth.

We can afford to wait.

God, the First and the Last

God is always first, and God will surely be last.

To say this is not to draw God downward into the stream of time and involve Him in the flux and flow of the world. He stands above His own creation and outside of time; but for the convenience of His creatures, who are children of time, He makes free use of time-words when referring to Himself. So He says that He is Alpha and Omega, the beginning and the ending, the first and the last.

Man in the plan of God has been granted considerable say; but never is he permitted to utter the first word nor the last. That is the prerogative of the Deity, and one which He will never surrender to His creatures.

Man has no say about the time or the place of his birth; God determines that without consulting the man himself. One day the little man finds himself in consciousness and accepts the fact that he is. There his volitional life begins. *Before* that he had nothing to say about anything. *After* that he struts and boasts and utters his defiant proclamations of individual freedom, and encouraged by the sound of his own voice he may declare his independence of God and call himself an "atheist" or an "agnostic." Have your fun, little man; you are only chattering in the interim between *first* and *last;* you had no voice at the first and you will have none at the last. God reserves the right to take up at the last where He began at the first, and you are in the hands of God whether you will or not.

This knowledge should humble us and encourage us, too. It should humble us when we remember how frail we are, how utterly dependent upon God; and it should encourage us to know that when everything else has passed we may still have God no less surely than before.

Adam became a living soul, but that becoming was not of his own volition. It was God who willed it and who executed His will in making Adam a living man. God was there first. And when Adam sinned and wrecked his whole life God was there still. Adam did not know it perhaps, but his whole future peace lay in this—that God was there *after* he had sinned. The God who was there at Adam's beginning remained there at his ending. God was there last.

It would be great wisdom for us to begin to live in the light of this wonderful and terrible truth: God is the first and the last. The remembrance of this could save nations from many tragic and bloody decisions. Were notes written by statesmen against the background of such knowledge they might be less inflammatory, less arrogant; and were kings and dictators to think soberly of this great truth they might walk more softly and speak less like gods. For after all they are not really important and the sphere of their freedom is constricted more than they dream.

Shelley tells of the traveler who saw in the desert two vast and trunkless legs of stone, and near them half-buried in the sand lay a shattered face with a "wrinkled lip and sneer of cold command." On the pedestal where once the proud image had stood were engraven these words: "My name is Ozymandias, king of kings: Look on my works, ye mighty, and despair." And, says the poet, "Nothing else remains. Round the decay of that colossal wreck, boundless and bare the lone and level sands stretch far away."

Shelley was right except for one thing: Something else *did* remain. It was God. He had been there first to look in gentle pity upon the mad king who could boast so shamelessly in the shadow of the tomb; and He was there when the winds of heaven blew down the statue and by the swirling sands covered with a mantle of pity the evidence of human decay. God was there last.